MEMOIRS OF A CHINESE
REVOLUTIONARY

Topical Press

DR. SUN-YAT-SEN

MEMOIRS OF A CHINESE REVOLUTIONARY

A Programme of National Reconstruction
for China

by

SUN-YAT-SEN

WITH A FRONTISPIECE PORTRAIT OF THE AUTHOR

AMS PRESS
NEW YORK

Reprinted from the edition of 1927, London
First AMS EDITION published 1970
Manufactured in the United States of America

Library of Congress Catalog Card Number: 73-111786
SBN: 404-06305-5

AMS PRESS, INC.
NEW YORK, N. Y. 10003

PREFACE

FOR thirty-one years I have toiled hard for the welfare of the Chinese people. My life has been consecrated to the Chinese people, and my devotion to the tasks I set myself has remained unchanged during this long period. Neither the might of the Manchu dynasty nor all the misfortunes of my life availed to turn me aside from the aims I placed before me. I strove for what I aspired to : and the more failures I experienced, the more I yearned for the struggle. That is why I was able to raise the mass of the Chinese people to revolutionary action, and thereby overthrow the monarchy and found the Republic.

At first it seemed as if I, as the leader, would be able very easily to give effect to the programme of the revolutionary party, i.e. nationalism, democracy, Socialism and the Fivefold Constitution, as well as solve the problems created by the Revolution. If I had succeeded in achieving this, China would have found her place amongst the family of nations and would have entered the path of progress and happiness. But, unfortunately, the Revolution was scarcely completed when the members of our party unexpectedly turned out to be of a different opinion from myself, considering my ideals too elevated and unattainable for the reconstruction of modern China.

These doubts, moreover, were taken for granted, and even some of my comrades began to entertain doubts concerning the realisation of my programme. Therefore it turned out that my programme had less chances of being realised when I held the post of President than when I was the leader of the Party which was preparing the Revolution. Hence the attempt at reconstruction was not successful, and the national tasks, which I put forward, were abandoned after the Revolution.

The Chinese Revolution, in the minds of many, was called upon to overthrow the Manchu dynasty and replace it by the tyranny of a group of bandits even more savage and rapacious than the former Tai-tsing Government. This was the direct cause of the further intolerable yoke that cast a shadow over the Chinese people. If we analyse our first promptings to carry out the Chinese Revolution, we shall see that we had in view the salvation of the Chinese people and the country ; whereas the result has been quite the opposite, and the Chinese people is becoming more and more oppressed, the country more and more unhappy.

To a considerable extent this results from my inability to influence my party comrades and, apparently, my incapacity to guide them. But, on the other hand, my party comrades also cannot escape the reproach of insufficient conviction and effort in the realisation of our revolutionary ideals and the carrying out of our revolutionary programme. As for the causes of their loss of heart, they do not all spring from the temptation of place and profit : their efforts slacken rather from their mode of thought.

What was that wrong mode of thought? It was, in their understanding, the idea that " actions are difficult, but knowledge is easy." This view was first expressed by Fu-Kueh, under the Emperor Wu-Ting of the Shan dynasty, two thousand years ago. Since that time it has taken root so deep in the mind of the Chinese people that now it is seemingly difficult to tear out. My whole plan for the reconstruction of China was paralysed by this saying.

When the first revolutionary wave went by, and organic reconstruction had to begin, I could not help being agitated and delighted, because at last I had united the ideal which had long matured within me with my plan of revolutionary action, in a programme of national reconstruction for China. I desired immediately to give effect to my programme, in the hope of leading China up the steps of progressive modern science. But there were already people to say to me : " We all recognise that your ideal is lofty and full of merit, and your plan is profound and all-embracing. But do you know that actions are always difficult, while knowledge is always easy ? "

When I first heard this I was dumbfounded and much confused, because I myself, like other Chinese, believed in this theory, and considered it indubitable that our ancient scholars taught us the truth. However, a little later I made up my mind to test this principle and overcome this obstacle. It turned out that my object was easily attainable. I inspired my comrades with the doctrine of Wang-Yuan-Ming, which preaches " unity of action and knowledge," i.e. the theory that knowledge is action and action knowledge.

But in time I discovered that the bold mind of the Chinese revolutionaries could not outstrip their courage. The whole Chinese people was in the same position. Later I devoted myself to the study of the question of " difficulty of action and easiness of knowledge." I studied this question for several years, and finally came to the conviction that the old tradition was false : the exact opposite is the case. I was happy because I had understood the cause of China's stagnation. It is due to the fact that the Chinese are ignorant of many things, and not at all because they cannot act.

The fact that, even though they have knowledge, they do not act, is due to their misconception that knowledge is easy but action difficult. Imagine that we can prove the opposite, and force the Chinese to act fearlessly. Without doubt the affairs of China will move forward considerably. Therefore I shall try to prove it by a number of

8

PREFACE

examples, in order to confirm the theory of the
easiness of action and the difficulty of knowledge ;
which may serve, on the one hand, for the subject
of discussion by scholars, and, on the other hand,
may teach the people to forget undesirable and
harmful traditions and superstitions.

The theory of the difficulty of action and the
easiness of knowledge came to us two thousand
years ago, and was accepted all over the country.
In the minds of a people of 400 millions it has
struck such deep roots that they cannot be torn
up without great effort. If we merely tell the
Chinese that it only seems to be the truth, but in
reality is a pure invention, it is hardly likely that
we shall convince them.

The theory of Fu-Kueh is my enemy, a thousand
times more powerful than the authority of the
Manchu dynasty. The power of the Manchus
could achieve only the killing of our bodies, but
it could not deprive us of our will. The might
of the theory of Fu-Kueh not only destroyed the
iron will of my comrades, but deceived the
millions of the Chinese people. During the time
of the Manchu dynasty, when I was agitating for
the Revolution, I could hope for progress, but in
the days that followed the establishment of the
Republic my plans for the reconstruction of China
could in no way be carried out. My thirty years'
faithfulness to my ideal was almost crushed by
this blow, my iron will almost killed. It was
terrible and hateful.

9

" The best method of struggle is to kill the mind."
So ancient military strategy teaches us. That is
why the national programme of reconstruction of
our Party suffered from the blow inflicted on our
minds by the enemy. The nation is an assembly
of individuals, and individuals, in their turn, are
receptacles of mind. Thus the affairs of the
people are the result of the expressions of mind
in groups of these individuals. While we believe
in our minds in the practicability of any plan, be
it to move mountains or to fill up the sea, it can
be easily accomplished. But when we are convinced in the impracticability, even of such
simple acts as to move our hand or to break a
twig, they cannot be carried out. Truly, great
is the power of mind.

Mind is the beginning of everything that
happens in the world. The overthrow of the
monarchy was carried out by mind, the construction of the Republic was delayed and later brought
to nought by this same mind. Just at the beginning
of the victory of the Chinese Revolution, the
revolutionaries themselves became the slaves of
the theory of the difficulty of action and the
easiness of knowledge, began to look on my plan
as a Utopia and empty words, and renounced
responsibility for the reconstruction of China.
That responsibility, of course, was not to have been
their monopoly, but should have been borne by
all the citizens of China. But seven years have
passed since the foundation of the Chinese

Republic, and literally nothing has been done in this direction. On the contrary, the affairs of the Chinese Republic have become more and more complicated and the difficulties of the Chinese people have grown with every passing day. When I think of this, day after day, my heart aches. The reconstruction of China cannot be postponed day after day. The question arises in my mind : " Chinese, why do you not carry out that which should and must be carried out— since, postponing it, you only obstruct your fulfilling your own appointed task ? Why is this ? Is it because you do not wish to fulfil it ? Or is it because you are incapable of grappling with it ? " I think that this arises, not because the Chinese are incapable, not because they have no inclination, but simply because they do not know it. When they become aware of it, the work of reconstruction will be just as easy as the turning of a hand or the breaking of a twig.

When I recalled all that I had taught the members of our Party, and what they had contemned : when I saw that my teaching was again coming to the surface as a new current in modern thought, and might become a plan for the national building-up of China, I conceived the purpose of writing a book about it under the title of *A Programme of National Reconstruction for China*, in the hope that my teaching would be accepted by all Chinese. However, I waited.

I feared that the psychology of the Chinese masses was the same as the psychology of our Party. Perhaps the Chinese still hold the opinion that actions are difficult but knowledge easy? If so, the result of my book and my teaching will be the same as seven years ago : they will look on my plan, on my programme for the reconstruction of China, as a Utopia.

However, I still begin the writing of this book, first of all for the purpose of crushing the enemy with the help of my theory, and leading the thoughts of my Chinese fellow-countrymen out of the blind alley in which they are at present. Then they will not look on my programme as a Utopia, and millions of them will be my sympathisers, will fight for the reconstruction of China, will consolidate the Republic, and will create a Government by the people, of the people and for the people. I believe in this, since I believe in the Chinese people.

SUN-YAT-SEN

Shanghai,
December 30, the 7th Year of the Republic (1918).

CONTENTS

PREFACE. THE CAUSES OF CHINA'S STAGNATION   PAGE 5

CHAPTER
I. THE MISTAKE OF THE CHINESE SAGES

(a) First Proof. Labour and Money . . 15
(b) Second Proof. The Problem of Human
Diet 38
(c) Third Proof. The Writing of Chinese . 57

II. "TO UNDERSTAND IS DIFFICULT, BUT TO
ACHIEVE IS EASY" (SEVEN MORE PROOFS) 73

III. THE CHINESE NEED KNOWLEDGE AND REVOLU-
TIONARY ACTION 101

IV. PROBLEMS OF THE REVOLUTIONARY REORGAN-
ISATION OF CHINA 119

V. WHO WAS RIGHT? 147

VI. THE CAUSES OF CHINA'S POVERTY . . 161

VII. A PLAN FOR THE DEVELOPMENT OF CHINESE
INDUSTRY 176

VIII. THE REVOLUTION IS THE PATH TO THE RE-
GENERATION OF CHINA. (HOW THE KUOMINTANG
ORGANISED THE CHINESE REVOLUTION) . 184

APPENDIX
I. "SAN-MIN-CHU" (THE THREE PRINCIPLES) . 225

II. "THE FIVEFOLD CONSTITUTION" . . . 239

MEMOIRS OF A CHINESE REVOLUTIONARY

CHAPTER I

THE MISTAKE OF THE CHINESE SAGES

(a) *First Proof. Labour and Money*

LET us take the circulation of money, and examine it from the standpoint of proving my theory that " action is easy and knowledge difficult." Of course, the circulation of money is not something inborn in human nature, but is rather only a habit of human life, practised by all civilised people. We need money to purchase our daily food, clothes, etc. We need it at home and during a journey. We spend it daily, and find that quite natural. We know that we can be masters of everything, if we have money ; and, on the contrary, we shall find it hard to make both ends meet, and will be in very great difficulties, if we have no money. Therefore we all hunt after money, and begin to depend on it more and more as society becomes more civilised, industry more developed, and the utilisation of money more widespread and diversified. Human bliss, sorrow or pleasure—nearly everything is determined by the money question. Therefore belief in the all-powerfulness of money has taken deep root in the mind of man.

The relations between man and money are so close, the mode of its use is so universally accepted —yet I ask : " How many people are there who know what money is and what is its functional peculiarity ?"

I should like first of all, reader, to have a talk with you about what money is. There is an old definition that money carries out the functions of exchange (for commodities). The Western economists also say that money itself belongs to the category of commodities, and is capable of determining the two important peculiarities, first, exchange at the average value of a commodity, and, second, to be a measure of all commodities. The writer takes them into account, calls money " established (or conditional) value," and defines it as follows : " Money is the established value of all commodities."

In far-off times money in China was made of shells, silk, beads or pearls ; later on of gold, silver and copper. At the present time the most savage and uncivilised tribes and peoples have almost the same kind of money as we Chinese had in primitive times. Amongst the nomad peoples oxen and sheep were reckoned as money, in fishing countries fish and shells, in agricultural countries fruit and millet. In present-day Mongolia and Tibet it often happens that they use tea and salt as money. In short, there are many things in the world which may be counted as money, and each tribe reckons to be coin the thing which is most suitable for it.

Specialists on questions of money-circulation talk of money as a thing which can act as the best established value for all commodities, if it possesses the seven following important qualities : (1) if it is suitable and has value ; (2) convenience for transport ; (3) indestructibility ; (4) purity ; (5) constant price ; (6) easy divisibility ; (7) if it is easily distinguished from other things. A thing which possesses these seven qualities may be called the best possible to serve as money.

During the Chow dynasty in China gold was the best coinage, silver the second, and copper the third. When the Chien dynasty conquered and seized the throne of the Chow dynasty, a single coinage was established. They reckoned gold sterlings and copper cash as money, but deprived pearls and shells of value. After the Chow and Chien dynasties, the coinage was subjected to changes but never went beyond the bounds of the utilisation of gold, silver and copper, and the same applies to the coins of all modern civilised countries. Some countries introduce gold as the chief coinage, with silver and copper as auxiliaries, while others insist that silver should be the chief and copper the auxiliary.

The reason prompting all countries to recognise gold, silver and copper as money is their possession of the principal qualities of " established value."

From the foregoing it is clear that any commodity suitable for " established value " may be transformed into money, and gold is only one of the varieties of such a kind of commodity. But why has gold retained such power of attraction up to our times? The answer is that the importance and power of gold are drawn by the latter only from the process of exchange of commodities. If there were no process of exchange of commodities gold would be transformed into sand and dust. Even if there were commodities, but no trading, gold would also lose its significance.

In order to show this, we shall take two examples. Some score of years ago there was a great famine in the provinces of Shensi and Shansi, in consequence of which cannibalism was rife. Millions of people perished of this famine. Both these regions were famous for their fertility and abundance. Their population had vast sums of money, and the banks in both provinces were full of deposits, for the people of these provinces every year brought home large sums earned as wages in the other provinces. However, the drought came, and bad harvests for several years led to the exhaustion of food stocks. Yet the gold which had been collected did not diminish. Many of the starving possessed gold, but they could not get a single bushel of millet for millions of dollars, and were driven to death by starvation. As there were no commodities, gold was useless. Have you read *Robinson Crusoe*? Try and imagine yourself in a similar position. You have brought a vast sum of gold with you, and have been exiled to a desert island. You have landed on it. The birds chirped to greet you, the flowers were beautiful, the fruits in the forest and the streams in the rocks were delightful and accessible. The whole island belongs to you, and all its treasures are entirely at your disposal, to spend them as you wish. But if you are hungry, you must procure the fruit yourself ; when you are tortured by thirst, you must get water from the stream. Everything flourishes on this island, there is any amount of commodities in their raw state, but there is no trade—and therefore no need of gold. You live not by your gold, but by your labour. What is important in such a situation— gold or labour ? In this way the reason for which gold in civilised societies possesses such a magic effect is now clear and can be exhaustively studied.

I want to discuss the nature and importance of money. The world has never yet seen trade which could exist if there is no money. What is it, however, that leads us to utilise money and what drives us to occupy ourselves with trade ? We must consider this more closely in order to know all the secrets of the monetary system. Before we can discover what leads to the utilisation of money, we must consider it from the standpoint of the evolution of civilisation.

As we see, savage peoples at the present time live in deep valleys and remote mountains, gathered together in clans and tribes. They wear homespun clothes and feed on what they kill themselves. Although they live close to one another, they communicate with other tribes very little and rarely. Their customs are very like those described in our old books, being just as " simple and sincere." More developed peoples live in valleys and plains where the earth is fruitful, produce abundant, communications easy, which facilitates relations between the various tribes.

From the way matters stand at the present day we can judge of what was the case in days gone by. People then constituted families and tribes, and maintained themselves. When they became a little more civilised, they began to engage in barter. Even the most conservative scholars, such as How-Shien, who preached the doctrine of self-maintenance—weaving and ploughing ourselves —could not hold out against the current of events, and were forced to exchange hats or crockery for rice. Barter was the guiding thread to trade.

But the question is asked, what then is the difference between barter and trade ? The difference is this : barter is the exchange of commodity for commodity, while trade is the exchange of commodities for money. Before money appeared, barter existed. This barter arose out of the division of labour. As the fulfilment by one man or by one tribe of several different kinds of work at the same time might harm the work they did, division of labour was invented with the object of perfecting it. Agriculturists began to devote themselves exclusively to tilling the soil, weavers began to produce only cloth. In this way the productivity of labour increased and there was no loss of time. Thanks to this division of labour, productivity increased, and as a result there was a surplus product which could be used for barter.

Thus the period of barter represents a higher development than the period of self-maintenance. Yet nevertheless it was by no means the last word in the division of labour. People might become specialised, but they could not combine production and trade : i.e. to do simultaneously the work of a craftsman and a merchant. The agriculturist had to bring the surplus of his rice, the weaver the surplus of his cloth to the market for exchange with one another. The same was the case with the fisherman, hunter, woodcutter, blacksmith and, in fact, all craftsmen : they brought their surplus for exchange for what they required. Otherwise the possessors of these surpluses could only throw them away as unnecessary, while others who needed them would not know where to procure them.

When one man has to do simultaneously the work of a merchant, a tiller of the soil and a craftsman, it involves unproductive waste of time. Yet such a division of labour obliges the agriculturist or craftsman to assume the work of a trader. There are, besides this, many difficulties in this kind of exchange. A certain Mr. W. wrote a book about his journey through the Philippines, in which he tells how, when he went into the villages of savage tribes, he could not get a single piece of bread all day, because the savages did not know the use of money, while they did not require what he had prepared for barter.

People living in olden times, and savages to-day, often experience this difficulty, as is seen from the following circumstance. The agriculturist has a surplus of food and needs clothes : he goes to the man who makes clothes and asks him to exchange. But the latter does not need food, but requires sheep : he goes to the sheep-farmer and asks him to exchange a sheep for his clothes. But the sheep-farmer does not want such an exchange, because he requires crockery. He brings his sheep to the craftsman to exchange for crockery, but the craftsman wants food. He, in his turn, brings his crockery to the owner of foodstuffs, but the latter would like to get clothes.

This circle of wishes will crush all the tillers of the soil, craftsmen, sheep-farmers, weavers, etc. Each of them has his surplus and needs something else, but, because the wish of each does not fall in with the wishes of others, none of them receive satisfaction. This depends on the absence of a proper place, where they could all come together and carry out their exchange. Owing to the absence of such a market they waste a lot of labour both on production and on exchange, but with little results, and of course progress is delayed.

An old Chinese Emperor, named Shien-Lung, foreseeing this, taught the people to " asscmble in the market-place at midday." Thus people and commodities could be assembled. After the barter, people returned home satisfied. If a market is created, this lightens the difficulties of barter. As for the four people mentioned, they could have come together in the market-place at the same time and place, and seek what they required. They would exchange what they require and would leave satisfied. The market saves time and gives facilities for barter. From the moment the market is recognised, there are no more obstacles to barter.

The same occurs with the utilisation of money. Hence the author draws the conclusion that the method of " assembling in the market-place at midday " is the guiding thread to the utilisation of money. Some economists affirm that money arose from barter. This supposition is mistaken. They do not know that during the period of barter there existed a " value " for commodities, just as nowadays we have a value in the period of trade. During the period of trade, money serves as a value for all commodities, while in the period of barter

" assembly in the market-place at midday "
served, like money, as the measure of value.

A man might utilise this value, i.e. a convenient
opportunity, to secure benefits, while those who
could not do so underwent many difficulties.
Before money entered into use, the institution
facilitating exchange was " assembly in the market-
place at midday," so that his must be considered
as the cradle of the origin of money. Once there
was an " assembly in the market-place at midday "
exchange took place very easily, as many commodities were set out on view before the crowd.
At the same time this gave great economy of
human labour, and also aroused an increase in
the desire to buy.

Previously people exchanged only the most
necessary and essential commodities, now they
pay more attention to the exchange of elegant
articles. Before commodities were themselves
exchanged, they were exchanged even earlier for
elegant articles, and the latter exchanged in their
turn for commodities. Elegant articles, such as
shells, precious stones and pearls, began to
represent the value of commodities : such is the
origin of money. Thus at first money was not the
chief thing. But from the time that barter
developed into exchange, money began to play
an important part. As money is used in exchange
for a commodity, its possessor nowadays can go
to any trader and buy what he requires, avoiding
his double obligations as a trader and a craftsman.

In this way the appearance of money greatly lightens the difficulties of mankind, greatly increases the production of commodities, and is ten times as advantageous as " assembly in the market-place at midday." The development of mankind was hastened, and civilisation moved forward considerably, with the introduction of the circulation of money.

According to my researches, the introduction of the use of money took place after the " assembly in the market-place at midday," i.e. after the Emperor Shien-Lung. The use of money was known at the time of the Chow dynasty, when civilisation had already moved forward greatly. The interval between them was about two thousand years. But culture at that time was not only higher than in previous times, but even could not be surpassed by the following centuries. This was really the greatest progress, resulting from the utilisation of money. From this we may draw the conclusion that the use of money serves as a great factor in the growth of civilisation. Only thanks to circulation of money was humanity able to step forward from primitive times to modern civilisation.

Some thousands of years after the appearance of money, modern machines were invented. After this the human race went forward more quickly, and material conditions developed and flourished still more. Machines afford the possibility of subjecting natural forces to the power of man, and utilise them in place of hand labour. What previously could not be done with the strength of a man is now excellently fulfilled by machines. When we use machines to load heavy weights, they develop an effort with which can be compared only the strength of several thousand human hands. When we use them to transport goods, they can in one day carry great weights for many hundreds of miles. When we use machines, under the control of one man, for tilling the soil, they reap as much rye as will feed several hundred men. When we use them for weaving, they can under one man's management produce clothes for a thousand men, and so on.

This invention created an entire revolution in industry, and money gradually began to lose its force. Why? Before the invention of machines, world production was carried on by hand labour. The volume of trade was limited, the total quantity of commodities did not go beyond the bounds of the sphere of money. But when world production passed from hand to machine labour, which is carried on by the united forces of nature and man, production increased thousands of times, and the volume of trade correspondingly increased many times. This forced the nature of trade to change. Commercial accounts gradually began to be managed by means of credit obligations, which nowadays are driving out money.

This can be illustrated by the following examples. A merchant sends a ship from Canton, with goods to the value of 1,000,000 dollars, to Shanghai, sells them, and divides them into ten parts. He makes 1 per cent. profit on every part, i.e. 1000 dollars on each. All this is paid him in cash. If we reckon it up in dollars, each part will weigh 4950 lan.[1] Supposing he gathers them together. Then he goes to the market to buy other goods, in ten lots. Besides the despatch of goods from the seller to himself, he must forward to the seller a large quantity of dollars. The man sells his goods in ten lots, receives their equivalent in dollars : then he must buy goods and pay for all he received also in ten lots. This means the purest waste of time and energy, and moreover involves great risk.

Further, when trade is carried on by many merchants in one place, all their goods taken together are worth millions and billions of dollars, and their trading operations require too much time for their completion. The money which passes through the hands of these merchants will constitute enormous sums. The silver and gold accumulated on the market will not suffice for such trade. Therefore gold and silver in such conditions lose their value. The strength of money becomes exhausted, and its place is taken by credit obligations.

What is the value of bills and mortgages ? This can be easily understood even by one ignorant of commercial affairs. In the case of the Canton

[1] One lan equals 1⅓ ounce of silver.

merchant already mentioned, who shipped goods to the value of 1,000,000 dollars to Shanghai, he sold them in ten lots and made 1 per cent. profit. Therefore he received 1,010,000. But this means not 49,500 lan, but only sheets of paper. It means either a banknote, or the note of some financial house, the share of some company, or a bill. When he sold his lots of goods, the buying and selling was limited to ten sheets of paper. Apart from delivering the goods, they will never pay one another in gold. A merchant from Fukien, ordering goods in Shanghai, pays with the same paper. Therefore in such transactions goods to the value of millions are sold without there being any need to bring gold with one, and this means economy, by eliminating the necessity of the double transmission of the 49,500 lan from the seller to the buyer and back. This also preserves money from loss or accident. Need it be said that this facilitates trade, reduces the cares and time spent on commerce, and at the same time produces advantages for society ?

Hence in modern civilised states commerce is carried on by means of credit (bills and cheques). Gold must lose its power. If the Chinese people still superstitiously believe that the power of gold has not fallen, this very much resembles the way How-Shien, towards the end of the Chow dynasty, still believed in self-supporting economy. People do not yet know that from the moment there began " the assembly in the market-place at midday," self-supporting by mixed forms of labour was unnecessary. When money came into use, " assembly in the market-place at midday," in its turn, became obsolete. Since men began to use credit (bills and cheques), money also has become valueless.

In the first year of the Chinese Republic, when I proposed that gold be withdrawn from circulation and bank-notes be introduced to lighten the burden on the State finances and to develop industry, my audience shouted that this was impossible. During the last Great War some countries did away with gold and introduced paper money in place of it, i.e. exactly what the author proposed seven years ago. If paper money is set going in the proper way, it will fully replace the use of gold.

But some put forward this objection : during our Yuan and Ming dynasties, four hundred years ago, paper money was also issued, but thereby they only hastened their downfall and increased the poverty of the people. During the Civil War in the United States, their Government also issued paper money, and this produced the same result. What was the reason ? It was that they issued paper money in unlimited and excessive quantities, and this led to their downfall, as the total money issued constantly increased, while the quantity of commodities remained the same.

However, some ask, did not the Pekin Government[1] stop paying cash on its bonds ? Is not this

[1] The Government of Yuan-Shih-Kai (1912–1916).

the abolition of money ? Why were there not the results which you expect, but, on the contrary panic and hesitation ? We think it was because the Pekin Government, when publishing this decree, copied only part of the measures adopted in other countries. In other countries the Governments did not pay on bills or cheques in specie, but at the same time they did not accept specie. The Pekin Government acted otherwise. When publishing the decree, it thought that it would not pay in specie to the people, but that this did not exclude the possibility of not accepting the bank-notes it had issued itself. But this was only deceiving the people by worthless and valueless paper. That is why the Pekin Government fell.

When Great Britain stopped paying on account of her bills, her Government at the same time stopped accepting specie. Therefore even war costs, which amounted to 60 or 70 millions a day, were paid for in paper, which circulated ceaselessly on the market and which everyone was glad to use. This went on for several months. When the Government issued a national loan, it was also paid up in paper. Those who had specie had to exchange it for paper bank-notes in the banks to pay their taxes or purchase commodities, otherwise their specie would have been worthless. That is how Great Britain ceased paying in cash (specie). But the Pekin Government did not accept the paper it had issued itself. It discredited its own notes, and yet forced everyone to trust them and accept them. Is such a thing possible ? It is hardly likely that a skilful merchant, or even a bad broker, would do such a thing : yet it was done by a Government calling itself the representative of the people. This is equivalent to proclaiming oneself a bankrupt.

The Pekin Government is quite ignorant in the question of currency. Many people are distinguished by this failing, even though they sometimes spend a great deal of money. During the Han dynasty, which inherited the ruin of the Chien dynasty, all adults were in the army, old and weak men served in the supply corps, work was very difficult, and the financial position of China bordered on bankruptcy. The Government of the day decided that this was due to insufficiency of currency, and therefore began to stimulate the people to coin money. However, little by little it began to be disquieted by the overproduction of coined money, and finally was obliged to forbid it altogether. Of course, this was not a correct method of procedure. The wealth or poverty of a nation by no means depends on the quantity of money, but rather on the quantity of commodities and their wide circulation.

At the beginning of the Han dynasty, the latter's difficulties were connected with a lack of commodities, and later on became more acute owing to their insufficient circulation. Therefore San-Hen-Yang, the counsellor of the Emperor Wu-Ti of the Han dynasty, introduced the

measure of " the lowering of the prices of commodities " down to their nominal value, in order
then to release commodities for proper circulation.
Collecting them in a normal period, he threw his
reserve supplies into the market when prices rose,
and thus lowered prices again to their normal
value. When the need for some kind of commodity
was felt in a particular locality and this raised
its price in that locality : or when there was a
superfluity of some commodity and therefore its
price fell, he was able to transfer his supplies
from one place to another, in order thereby to
regulate commodity prices. He did this because
he knew the real meaning of money. It is a great
pity that these measures were not again introduced
after the time of San-Hen-Yang, as Chinese
national economy to-day more than ever is in a
chaotic and confused condition.

At the present day, after the outbreak of the
Great War, nearly the whole adult population in
the belligerent countries was called to arms.
Industry came to a standstill at this time, and the
value of money fell heavily. The Governments
of all belligerent countries were obliged to take
over a number of branches of industry and
commerce, and to adapt them for military purposes.
This was achieved first of all in Germany and
Austria, but other countries followed their example
immediately. This was in essence the policy of
San-Hen-Yang.

According to the teaching of European scientists,

human existence can be divided into three grades. The first represents requirements, the lack of which makes life insupportable. The second stage represents the conveniences, without which life is not quite pleasant. The third stage is luxury, which is not very essential to life. We increase our happiness if we possess it, but it does not destroy our convenience if we lose it. Naturally, if we study these stages in their application to humanity to-day, they will have a very elastic meaning. What one man considers a necessity, others will reckon an article of comfort, and yet others as a luxury. But if we speak of these stages with reference to various epochs, these differences stand out very sharply.

The writer considers that the times which preceded the use of money were the age of primary necessities. Human aspirations at that time did not go beyond the bounds of the desire to be well fed and clothed. People then did not strive for other things, and could not strive for them. From the moment that money came into use, there began the epoch which we can call the age of procuring the means for achieving comfort, because human desires were growing and could not be satisfied by food and clothing alone : the more because they could procure things which brought them comfort. From the time of the invention of machines begins the age of luxury. Only in this period can we observe over-production.

We do not fear poverty any more, but we are

afraid of inequality of distribution. Countries with a strongly developed industry try to extend their market, and to export their manufactured goods to countries with a less developed industry. Many civilised countries, unfortunately, maintain the nonsensical point of view that only articles of luxury bring benefit to mankind. Corresponding with the evolution of the three stages of economic development there takes place the evolution in the understanding of conditional value. In the age of primary necessity " assembly in the market-place at midday " afforded the possibility of exchange. In the age of comfort, money, which we still use, was current. In the age of luxury money is replaced by credit (cheques, bills).

These alterations in the conditional value of all three epochs are conducive to the happiness of mankind, and men should take advantage of them. But this does not mean that it is no use having recourse to other methods than those already existing. For example, in the days of " assembly in the market-place at midday," people still continued to conduct self-supporting economy. There were and are still people who practice " assembly in the market-place at midday " during the period of the utilisation of the monetary system, as for example, a fair which takes place every three days. This takes place in the neighbourhood of towns. Even before people reached the age of luxury, they already knew the use of bills (cheques), paid out in place of money, in

the shape of the so-called " flying bills " and
" money notes " of the Tan dynasty, and " notes
of hand " and " notes on call " during the Sun
dynasty. These were the forerunners of bills of
exchange. In our own times we have to use
bills (or cheques), otherwise we cannot carry on
industry or commerce on a large scale. But it
is possible at the same time to use money, even
though this be not so convenient and advantageous
as cheques.

China is now living through the second stage of
economic development. Agriculture and handicrafts are still served by hand labour. She has
not yet reached the stage of utilising machines,
and thus harnessing the forces of nature to help
hand labour, by the application of steam, gas,
electricity and water-power. Nevertheless, with
the opening of port trade with other countries,
our economic activity has greatly increased. This
is not because the foreign merchants have more
money than we, but because the quantity of im-
ported goods exceeds the quantity exported by
us : the difference amounts to two milliard
dollars a year. In ten years it will amount to
twenty milliards. If this goes on, the damage
will be irreparable, even if we had piles of gold
as high as mountains, and innumerable and
bottomless copper mines. We know well that
the day will come when our poverty will reach
its culminating point, and our wealth will disappear. What is the way out ? The one and only

way out of such a condition is the introduction of machinery.

When we examine the yearly incomes of industrial countries and divide them by the number of the population, we see that every citizen can receive seven hundred or eight hundred dollars, on the average, yearly. In our country, which still makes use only of hand labour, every person in the population would receive an average of seven or eight dollars of yearly income. But if we bring in machine production, we shall naturally be able to achieve the same results as characterise the industrial countries, and then those seven or eight dollars, i.e. our national wealth, will increase an hundredfold compared with the present time. We can then move on to a higher stage of economic well-being.

The industrial revolution in the European and American countries produced a sudden change in their living conditions. Their daily life rapidly entered the period of luxury and great creature comforts. Its effect on society is exactly similar to that which Henry George described in his book: *Progress and Poverty*. He said that the progress of modern civilisation is like a sharp wedge suddenly driven in between the upper and lower classes. Those who are above this sharp wedge are a small minority of capitalists. This minority is pushed up higher and higher by the wedge every day. Those who live below represent the vast majority of workers. They are dragged lower and lower every day. This means that the rich become richer, while the poor become ever poorer. The results of the industrial revolution bring happiness only to a few members of society, but inflict pain and suffering on the great part of the people. It is not surprising that the social revolutionary movement is growing, as it is natural that the majority cannot any longer be sacrificed to the luxurious life of the minority.

Why are such great losses and sufferings inflicted on humanity? Because people do not know how to adapt themselves to new conditions. During the supremacy of hand labour, the theory of *laissez-faire* prevailed, in order to encourage free competition, suppress the growth of monopolies and distribute income amongst the whole population. This was practised unconsciously for several thousand years. Only after Adam Smith, in the eighteenth century, discovered the truth at the bottom of all activity, did he express what everyone wanted to say but could not, and this brought him the respect of his contemporaries and even of the people of our own day.

About a century passed after the publication of *The Wealth of Nations* before the industrial revolution was fully developed. From that turning point onwards, humanity began to use machines for the extension of production. Those who possessed machinery were enabled to rule the world by reason of their weath. If we still retain the custom of free competition, or the method of *laissez-faire*, it will be like encouraging a lame man to contend with an automobile in a race. Even a child can see the impossibility of such a contest.

From the foregoing we can draw the conclusion that we cannot ascertain the laws governing currency if we do not study the evolution of civilisation and understand the development of the monetary system. We also cannot know these laws if we do not carefully study the history of commerce and industry, banking, the origin of money, etc. In short, the majority of European and American citizens, like the Chinese, unfortunately, only know the power of money. Apart from this, they are quite ignorant of the laws of currency. They are inclined to think that money is founded on commodities. Only Socialists can understand that money is founded on human labour (including all hand and brain labour). Thus power rests in human labour and not in money.

And so I say that people unfortunately know only how to spend money, but very rarely understand its secrets. This is the first proof of my theory that " action is easy but knoweldge difficult."

(b) Second Proof. The Problem of Human Diet

Let us take another example—human diet. This is a very important function of our organism. At the same time it is a function which every living creature can carry out. A child which has left its mother's womb, a chick which has broken out of the egg can carry it out equally well without being specially trained. But when we reflect and ask ourselves, do we fully know the secret of this, then not only cannot the man in the street reply in the affirmative, but, even after the remarkable discoveries and inventions of modern science, not a single physiologist, doctor, hygienist, physicist or chemist, even after devoting their whole lives to the study of this question, and whether they lived a hundred years ago or at the present day, can fully grasp all its significance.

Our China, although backward and imperfect in everything, has not been outdone by a single country in the development of the art of preparing various kinds of food. The dishes prepared by the Chinese surpass those of the European countries as much as do our methods of cookery. As for the taste of the Chinese, the newest and most up-to-date principles invented by Western doctors and hygienists cannot surpass the Chinese. Let us leave aside such dishes as are out of the ordinary, the so-called "eight delicacies." But as regards dishes of daily use, such, for example, as "Chien-Chen," bean jelly and kidney beans, these are the best form of vegetable dish, but Europeans do not even know that they can be used as food at all. Dishes made of the giblets and internal organs of domestic animals were always reckoned dainties amongst the Chinese; the Americans and English formerly did not eat them, but now do so.

In Canton I met a foreigner who despised us as savages and barbarians, because we eat black-puddings. But a doctor has ascertained that pig's blood is composed of a mass of ingredients containing iron, which is an excellent means for the restoration of energy. All Western people who formerly were given purified iron after illness, child-birth or anæmia, now take black-puddings instead of iron, because the ferrous compounds which they contain are of organic origin, and more convenient for physical health than purified inorganic iron. Thus black-puddings, used as a food, can serve both to strengthen a sick man and to benefit a healthy man ; and the Chinese, who use it as a food, are not barbarians or savages, but enlightened and hygienic people. This is only one example, but a great number might be quoted. A number of dishes, prepared by the Chinese but quite unknown to Western countries—such as " Yen-Okh " (swallows' nests) and " Yu-Chih " (fins)—are considered the most delightful food by the Chinese, while Western peoples can only wonder that they can be used as such.

If painting, which pleases the eyes, and music, which pleases the ears, can be considered arts, then such undoubtedly can also be considered delicacies which please the palate. Therefore the preparation of food in its way is an art. The French are considered the best cooks in Western countries, and it is in France that we find the highest civilisation. Hence we learn that good methods of preparing food are produced by civilisation : and this is natural. A people untouched for a long time by civilisation is incapable of distinguishing the most delicate flavours, and if there is no fine distinction of flavours, there will be no skilful cookery. The skilful preparation of food by the Chinese will be a sufficient indication of the astounding progress of Chinese civilisation.

In times when there was no commerce between China and Western countries, the Western peoples knew that France was famous for the best cookery in the world. But when they learned of Chinese cookery, they began to admire the Chinese. The first Western person who travelled in our interior provinces was the Portuguese Matthew Ricci. During the reign of our Emperor Yao-Huang, of the Ching dynasty, he travelled through many provinces on his way to Tibet. In his reminiscences of his journey he more than once extolled Chinese civilisation, writing with particular enthusiasm about our cooking.

In recent years, when Chinese appeared abroad, Chinese cookery became, in some sort, fashionable. In New York alone the number of Chinese restaurants reaches some hundreds. There is no American town without a Chinese restaurant.

The Americans seek after Chinese cookery like madmen, so much so that the professional American cooks envy Chinese very much. They spread various rumours to the effect that the bean sauce used by Chinese contains poisons which are destructive of human health. Convinced by this invention, one municipal council issued an order that Chinese were on no account to make bean sauce. Later on, medical researches established that bean sauce not only contains no poisons, but contains many nutritive ingredients, similar to those in meat juice. They not only inflict no harm upon the body, but on the contrary are very beneficial. The prohibition was withdrawn.

Chinese cooking is widespread not only throughout America, but also in Europe, where there are now many Chinese restaurants in the large towns. Since the reforms in Japan, the Japanese copy Western civilisation in everything; nevertheless, so far as cooking is concerned, they still prefer the Chinese methods. To-day there are many Chinese restaurants in Tokio.

Not only are there many dishes invented by the Chinese, and the skilful preparation of food generally, which cannot be surpassed by other countries, but Chinese taste also, unconsciously coinciding with the rules underlying the modern principles of science and hygiene, is above all praise. In China the common people drink aristocratic green tea, while their food is a rice dish with vegetables and bean jelly. This kind of food, so hygienists tell us, is the most valuable for the health. This is confirmed by the fact that people living in remote districts, without wine and meat, reach an advanced age. The fact that the Chinese survive plague and other diseases is partly attributable to the fact that the Chinese food unconsciously conforms to the rules of hygiene. Therefore the Chinese can undertake the serious study of the science of hygiene, and try to master it. This will certainly strengthen the Chinese people even further in comparison with its present position.

The Western advocates of a vegetarian diet rely on their knowledge of hygiene for their claim that it prolongs life. But as their range of dishes is not so ample and attractive, and their seasonings are not as good as ours, they often undermine their health by insufficient nourishment even while enthusiastically advocating vegetarian food. Hence vegetarianism is scarcely likely to become widespread. Chinese vegetarians must eat bean jelly, since this is nothing else than so-called " vegetarian meat." It has all the qualities of meat, but is free from its poisons. Yet the Chinese have become accustomed to it without the aid of science.

The Europeans drink sour wines and eat tainted meat. They have become so accustomed to this that they cannot alter it, although there exist amongst them drastic penal laws, prohibiting the sale of wines (as in America and Russia), and also new discoveries in the sphere of hygiene. Luckily, in respect of eating and drinking, we have acquired much better habits than any other countries. In distinction from other nations, we have acquired these good habits without encouragement or intimidation. We must always retain them, in order to set an example to the whole world.

The ancient sages used to say that man is " the universe in miniature," but we should rather say that he is a " little State," since the stomach and intestines, with their appropriate functions, really resemble State institutions transacting the affairs of their country. As for the various parts of the body, the perfection of their organism and the rapidity of their action are quite unattainable by State institutions. And all these secrets of life are very far from being understood as yet by modern knowledge.

Researches of modern scientists show that the material of which the human being and all living things are composed is nothing else than cells, i.e. living atoms. But what is a cell? It is a very small object, very surprising and extremely mysterious. According to the discoveries of modern science, it is very sensitive and intelligent. It can act, move and think. It has reasons and intentions. What is it that makes our body so extraordinary, astonishing and mysterious, if not this cell?

THE MISTAKE OF THE CHINESE SAGES

Various phenomena in the animal and vegetable world are expressions of the exchange and combination of cells. While humanity builds its houses, ships, carriages, towns and bridges, the cell creates humanity and all other living objects. Birds in the air are aeroplanes created by cells. Scaly fish in the water are submarines created by cells. What people call instinct and intuition are also the instinct and intuition of cells. Since modern scientists discovered that cells are sensitive, which the old philosophers could not understand, much can now be explained. A new era has now begun, for knowledge has greatly widened the limits of our understanding.

The human body is created by cells : the organs functioning like the digestive system are cell factories. The food which man eats becomes the food of cells. While man lives on the earth, cells are bound up with him. Cells joined together in different parts of the body are like people living in different towns. The very first condition for human existence is to be fed and clothed : the same applies to cells. Therefore the first and chief requirement of cells is fuel and materials. Eight-tenths of what we eat are consumed as fuel, while the remainder is utilised as restorative materials.

The fuel has two purposes. One is to warm the body : this is comparable to the fact that men burn wood to protect themselves against cold. The other purpose is to do the same as burning coal in the stokehold of a factory boiler, namely, to produce energy and transform it into power. As a man who works requires more power, he eats more than a man who works little and therefore requires less power. If there is more than sufficient food to supply him with heat the surplus will be used in the storing-up of fat for unforeseen circumstances. If there is insufficient heat, the cells must extract the fat already stored, and use it as fuel. If the fat has been used up, it has to be drawn out of the body and muscles. This is the reason why a man who has not sufficient food is inclined to be thin and emaciated.

Foodstuffs serve at the same time to supplement the cells needed for building up the body. If there are more materials than are required, they are all transformed into heat and are not stored up in the body. This is very similar to the way in which surplus building materials in the towns are burned for fuel, as not otherwise required. Thus there should not be an excess of food, otherwise it will swallow up the energy of many organs in transforming it into heat. In the event of the food being unsuitable for fuel, the remnants of the burning will waste the energy of the kidneys in their elimination. The kidneys will be overtired and therefore damaged. Therefore it is extremely undesirable to have an excess of food.

Food can be divided into two categories—the first, as a kind of fuel: this is the distinguishing feature of vegetables; the second as reconstructing materials : these abound in meat. If there is an excess of these reconstructing materials, they can be used up as fuel : but, on the other hand, if there is an excess of fuel, it cannot be turned into reconstructing material. Therefore an insufficiency of such materials cannot be permitted, as it would mean the destruction of the intestines and stomach. If men know these elementary truths, the preservation of health and the prolongation of life will gain greatly.

Food usually consists of several most important elements : nitrogen, carbohydrates and fats. In addition, there are also water, salt, iron, phosphorus, magnesium and organic compounds (chemists have not yet discovered what elements constitute the latter), which are necessary to man. In 1 gramme of nitrogen there are 4·1 calories of heat : in 1 gramme of carbonic acid, 4·1 calories : in 1 gramme of fats, 9·3 calories. In domestic animals and fish there is much nitrogen. In vegetables there is also nitrogen, particularly in beans.

As for the amounts which a man must consume daily, here physiologists differ. Some affirm that 100 grammes of proteids are sufficient, others say that 50 are enough. One Austrian physiologist found that every kilogramme of the body required from 34 to 40 calories when a man is engaged on mental work, while from 40 to 60 calories are required by a man engaged in physical work. Therefore a man weighing 70 kilogrammes requires

2800 calories in the first case and 3500-4000 calories in the second.

But another scientist who tested this drew a somewhat different conclusion. He weighed 86 kilo, ate 45 grammes of proteids daily and 1800 calories of fuel in addition. Then, although his weight diminished by 13 kilo, he nevertheless felt more vigorous and strong. Then he reduced the proteids to 38 grammes and the fuel to 1500 calories, but still remained the same as before. Many physiologists are now making experiments concerning how many grammes of food a man must consume. According to their opinion, there must be not less than 50-100 units of nitrogen, which a man requires for the rebuilding of his body. There must be not less than 3000-4000 calories of fuel. Cases when a man, engaged in very heavy labour, requires five or six thousand calories are very rare.

The illnesses of man usually arise from insufficient care for his nourishment. In the animal world, all animals are guided by their instinct, they are entirely under the control of their requirements, and therefore the quantity of their food reaches only certain limits. When the limit has been reached, they will not eat any more. In far-off times men also acted in this way, and savage tribes untouched by modern civilisation still act in the same way, because they have not yet lost their nature, and their capacity for satisfaction is still limited. Hence they rarely yield to the passion for eating. It is otherwise

THE MISTAKE OF THE CHINESE SAGES

with civilised people. The higher the civilisation, the more the evil is developed (wine, opium and much else that is harmful to the health), and unsatisfied desires grow in the measure that civilisation develops. Hence it is not surprising that we have a vast number of people suffering from lack of control of their nourishment.

The writer also once suffered from an illness which was the consequence of overloading the stomach. The beginning was very slight, but I let the illness develop, as I was busy with other matters. However, it proved very serious. I began to receive treatment. The illness subsided, and I gave up treatment, as other matters again distracted my attention. For some time my malady remained stationary, but in the course of time medicines and pills ceased to help, and I was forced to turn my attention seriously to the state of my health. I ate only boiled rice, meat extract and milk. At first this greatly assisted me, but did not cure me completely, and this remained my condition for six months. Then the sickness grew worse, the pain in my stomach was constant, until there was no medicine which could help me to cure it.

Then I altered the method of treatment, and had recourse to massage. At first this gave satisfactory results : however, in a few months the old malady again asserted itself, and grew worse and worse. I tried to find a doctor acquainted with medicine and surgery. I met a Japanese, Mr. K. The

D   49

method of this doctor is undoubtedly excellent He has written a book entitled *On the Maintenance of Health by the Method of Resistance*, in which he recommends a method of nourishment quite opposite to the ordinary. The Western doctors order easily digestible foods for the sick man, and instruct him to avoid heavy or compact foods. Whereas Mr. K. advises you to avoid both meats and liquid food, such as milk, boiled rice, eggs and meat juice, but to eat hard vegetables and fresh green leaves, selecting those which are easily digested, in order to arouse the stomach and intestines and increase their activity, and thus return to them their natural functions.

At first I did not believe in this, but later when I reflected that I had been taking milk and boiled rice for six months without results, why should I not try this method of healing? Moreover observing that Mr. K.'s methods had already relieved my discomfort, I resolved to follow his advice. Mr. K. said: "Healing is only a temporary cure; if you want to free yourself completely of your illness, the root of the evil, you must maintain your health by the method of resistance." I followed his advice, and the methods he suggested, and achieved satisfactory results.

A few months after my recovery, when I again ate eggs, milk, tea, etc., my old trouble returned to me. At first I thought that this was due to other causes, unconnected with my diet, but three or four times it led to the same consequences, and I was obliged to carry out exactly the instructions of Mr. K., completely avoiding meat, eggs, milk and every kind of irritant food. I eat boiled rice, vegetables and a little fish. My illness has gone these last two years. My diet has made my body as strong as it was formerly. After taking food I do not experience any feeling of overloading, but, on the contrary, I feel very well. This I did not experience before : it has happened only during these last two years.

I studied in a school of medicine, and thought myself well grounded in physiology and hygiene. But I despised my own hygiene in small things and acquired a stomach ailment which was almost incurable. I was lucky enough to learn from Mr. K. how to maintain my health by the method of resistance, thanks to which I was enabled, at length, to get rid of my sickness of long standing. The theory of Mr. K. is truly a great discovery in medical science. From this we also can see *how difficult it is to know the right method of nourishment.*

Moreover, different people have different natures, and this, of course, must be taken into consideration before prescribing for anyone a specific diet. A thing which is suitable for one man may not suit another. In the same way the method of curing various illnesses cannot be uniform or generalised. But generally the rules for taking food and maintaining one's health cannot be other than to eat in good time and not to eat to excess.

These elementary principles must be observed by every man. Meat, which enters into our dietary, is intended first of all to create heat in the body and to facilitate the formation of its tissues. Vital energy also depends on meat. This is very important, and cannot be overlooked. But the quantity which a man must eat must be proportionate to the size of his body. In accordance with the foregoing, too much food must not be taken, otherwise it only causes harm to the body. Many cases are known in which an excessive quantity of meat has brought harm to the body. The quantity must be varied according to age. Young people, who still have to grow, can eat more than adults, while an old man must eat less.

That vegetarian food is the best for the prolongation of life has been recognised by all scientists, hygienists, physiologists and doctors. But in addition it should be recognised that the Chinese method of preparing food from vegetables is the best. Bean jelly must be regarded as meat, and in its use we should not exceed the quantity required by a man. When estimating the quantity of this food which a man can eat, it is necessary to follow subjective hygiene as closely as possible.

What changes does food undergo during its digestion in the stomach, i.e. how does it change when the stomach and intestines transform it into blood ? These secrets are even more difficult to clear up than the problems of diet. When food enters the mouth, it must first of all pass the test of the tongue, in order that we can discover whether it is suitable for the stomach, and whether it can be digested. If it is not accepted by the stomach, nausea at once arises and it is thrown out. If it is suitable, the tongue accepts it and mixes it with saliva, the teeth chew it and break it up, the saliva helps to soften and moisten it, in order to transform the starch into sugar.

When the process has been completed in the mouth, the food is conveyed with the help of the tip of the tongue through the gullet into the stomach. The passage expands and carries it to its destination. When the food enters the stomach, the lower end of the stomach immediately closes, and the stomach distributes the food within itself. If it is satisfied, its cells immediately inform the brain, and the latter in turn gives the order to stop eating. That is why we often feel satisfied after food. This is one of the functions of the stomach, as it establishes the quantity of food we require day by day. When we feel satisfied, we must stop eating, otherwise we only hurt the well-being of our body.

When the food has been supplied, the juices of the stomach begin softening the proteids in exactly the same way as saliva softens the starch. The muscles of the stomach contract and expand alternately, expanding and squeezing the food until it becomes a paste. Then the stomach opens its lower end and shifts the food to the intestines ; here it is mingled with the intestinal juices. What the saliva and stomach juices have been unable to dissolve is dissolved by the intestinal juices. The food then passes into the liver. What is valuable for the body is transferred to the heart, whence it is carried by the arteries and distributed over the various parts of the body to feed the tissues. What is useless for the body is immediately rejected by the liver and not allowed to enter the blood. Then it passes through the gall-bladder to the small intestines again, to produce the juices necessary for secretion. Finally, the useless remnants and refuse pass into the larger intestine, where they accumulate to the necessary quantity and are thrown out as excrement. This is the whole process of nutrition. Much can still be said of what happens to the transformed food which enters the blood. But this cannot be understood by persons who have not studied physiology, and even physiologists are not fully acquainted with the process.

All that has been said above refers to the internal structure of the digestive system and the process of nutrition. This is a natural phenomenon, yet it can be said that to grasp all its important features is very difficult. Let us now consider such questions as the production of food, its transport and distribution, and the prevention of famine, which are the direct result of man's intervention, and also cannot be studied simply and easily.

Social policy in modern countries reached its highest state of organisation in Germany. During the great Imperialist war, Germany was blockaded by Great Britain at sea. It might have been expected that the German people would be left without food supplies. The panic amongst the Germans was general. The population suffered many hardships. But two years after the war began the German Government applied scientific methods to the problem of food supply. Germany emerged from the food crisis, and the panic ceased. This gave Germany the means of holding out in isolation another two years : without this, Germany would have had to surrender immediately to the Allies.

Up to that time, the German people, when wishing to buy food, had had to stand in queues awaiting their turn. Many policemen were required to maintain order. The shopkeepers supplied their goods to the purchasers in the order of their coming. When supplies gave out, those at the back of the queue returned empty-handed. Thus those who desired to receive food had to give up their sleep for the preceding night, go to the shop, and there wait for the queue until dawn. One German doctor said very wittily, that, if a German woman slept six hours longer in her flat, she would have more fats in her body than she was able to buy.

Hence it is not difficult to imagine the state of affairs in Germany at that time. The methods introduced by the German Government were none other than socialisation and careful utilisation. If we look at the previous food production of Germany, we shall see that it could support 80 per cent. of the people, while, improved in the way indicated, it could be increased by more than 20 per cent. Therefore the first decision of the German Government was to prohibit extravagance in foodstuffs and to limit excess. It introduced a method of distribution of foodstuffs by which everyone had a definite quantity of food daily. Thus the total quantity of food was not increased, but it was distributed amongst the people more or less satisfactorily. Moreover, production was increased. All parks and uncultivated lands, covered with grass, were given over to agricultural produce, and measures were adopted for the production of artificial manures. All that the German people had suffered, and that for the first two years they had looked upon as an incurable evil, was settled quite satisfactorily by this system of rational distribution. Poverty was levelled out, and necessary requirements moderately fulfilled. As for their achievements, they cannot be ascribed to the difficulty of action, but on the contrary, to the knowledge of how to act—which is acquired with great difficulty.

Summing up the foregoing, i.e. the process of digestion, consumption, purification, construction and destruction of the elements of food, which constitute the process of nutrition, the following conclusions can be drawn. If a man sees how raw materials are delivered to a factory and there worked up by machines and transformed into beautiful things, does this mean that he can say that all this was done by machines? Of course not. Why? Because there also exists human power, which controls the machines, and which must be taken into account. The unusual functions of various organs, which can be attributed to them, are not created by the organs themselves, but by the cells working within them. Hence we can draw the conclusion that the understanding of the process of nutrition is very difficult. Though the management of food supplies is practised by many citizens, nevertheless their rational distribution is not easily understood by everyone. This again shows that " knowledge is difficult, but action easy."

(c) *Third Proof. The Writing of Chinese*

Further we illustrate our theory by the art of writing books. In the course of several thousand years the Chinese have created a great literature. Everyone in China, beginning with emperors and kings and ending with the common people, even robbers and pirates, all have been able to value and delight in literature as an art. Through this excessive passion for literature, the Chinese look upon persons possessing this gift as all-powerful. Many talented and gifted persons have given up all other occupations in order to devote themselves entirely to the study of literature. This led to the result that every other kind of profession died out, and our country grew weak.

So far as our literature is concerned, we cannot but admit that it is exceptionally fine and full of value. Since the Chinese Emperor Fu-Shi wrote his " Eight Diagrams " in the most ancient times, the evolution of writing has continued for over 5000 years. Although not all of the 400 millions of the Chinese people can read and write, nearly all are under the direct or indirect influence of Chinese literature. Beyond the boundaries of our country, this influence extends over Japan, Korea and Indo-China, which consider themselves akin to the Chinese in their language.

If we speak of the length of time during which the Chinese language has been in use, we know that it has outlived the dead languages of Egypt, Rome, Babylon and Greece. If we speak of its geographical diffusion, and compare it with English—the so-called " most widely-adopted " tongue, which is spoken, as has been ascertained, by 200 million people—the Chinese language is twice as widely distributed, since it is spoken by 400 million people. When any people develops to the stage of having its own national literature, this is considered a great step forward. But even more important must be a literature which has been able to exert its influence over neighbouring countries, absorb them, or refashion them after its own likeness. This is shown by the fact that 5000 years ago our country occupied a tiny space in the valley of the Yellow River, whereas now it has become immeasurably the greatest country in the world. Although during the centuries China was often seized by foreign invaders, it was never swallowed up and enslaved by these nations, despite its weakness and powerlessness, but on the contrary the conquerors were assimilated by the Chinese as easily as the moving of a table. This can be ascribed only to the exceptional peculiarities of the Chinese language.

Some modern Chinese writers agitate for the abolition of Chinese letters and characters, but the author holds the opinion that the latter should under no circumstances be abolished.

The use of machines and money, as has been said above, helps mankind to achieve better (comfortable and luxurious) material conditions; but so far as intellectual progress is concerned, only to the language has it been given to continue and extend it. It is certain that material progress and intellectual civilisation mutually influence each other and wait each on the other in the common progress. The slow improvement of China's material conditions retards the aspirations of its intellectual civilisation. However, it does not therefore follow that we should give up the work of research in the sphere of ages long past. On the contrary, if we compare modern Chinese civilisation with the European, we shall see that, while we fall behind the Europeans in material conditions, yet in the sphere of intellectual development the Chinese have many achievements equal to those of the Europeans, and in some cases even more progressive. However, there are also those which cannot be compared with European literature.

Those are utterly wrong who wave Chinese civilisation aside with a stroke of the pen, without ever meditating on the matter. Further, the mode of thought and the ideals of the Chinese to-day, were all shaped by their forefathers. Consequently, when we now attempt to improve and alter various aspects of our life and manners, we must strive to study our ancient modes of thought and ideals, in order to ascertain the source and development of those ideals, to grasp their good and bad sides, and thus to understand them better. Only after such a careful study can we discover the way to correct the prejudices, the inclinations and the peculiarities which characterise the Chinese. And as written works are only the means and the intermediaries for the transmission of ideas, this quality of writing can be compared with the function of the monetary system, which plays the part of an intermediary in exchange. If we insist on the abolition of Chinese characters, how shall we approach the ancient mode of thought and study it ?

Furthermore, since the beginning of history,

these Chinese characters have told the story of all events which took place during these four or five thousand years, exactly and continuously. This is an exceptional peculiarity of the Chinese language. It should not only be appraised at its true worth by scholars, but also utilised by them. If it be utilised in the proper way, and if we make use of the ancient scholars, they will not lead us astray; if we utilise them instead of being enslaved by them, ancient chronicles and documents will help us to study the ancient scholars, who will serve as historians for us. And the more numerous they are, the better. European scholars are not afraid even of the dead characters of Egypt and Babylon (although those two countries perished long ago, and their tongues have long ago fallen into disuse). They are not afraid of collecting and studying even the fragments of the history of the past, and of restoring them, since they consider that the ideas of ancient times may be very useful for our modern knowledge.

In China the spoken and written languages are not at all identical. Of course, Chinese writing is founded on the spoken language. But the spoken language has undergone changes at different periods. So far as Chinese writing is concerned, however, although the manner of it has changed at various times, nevertheless these changes cannot be compared with the rapid alterations in the spoken language. Thus, in very far-off times, before our first " three dynasties," when our characters were only being formed, and the spread of Chinese culture was limited to the valley of the Yellow River, both speech and writing were identical : this cannot be gainsaid. By the time of the " Chow dynasty," culture had already spread far beyond the bounds of the Yellow River valley. The tribes of Hupeh, Hunan, Anhwei, Fukien and Kiangsu were under the influence of Chinese writing, but each still retained its local language, and this was the origin of the difference between written and spoken speech.

When the Chow dynasty began to decline, various savage tribes occupied the plains of China. Foreign languages began to be heard side by side with Chinese. A thousand years later, during the time of the " five dynasties " the Lian and Yunan dynasties, and again two thousand years later, i.e. in the period of the last Manchu dynasty, when the Mongols, Tibetans and Manchus were trying to seize China and were dominating the Chinese, the dialects of these tribes more or less left their impress on the Chinese language.

Three thousand years ago, during the Han dynasty, the Chinese sought to write the Chinese characters beautifully, but the spoken language was left to develop on its own. There were changes in conversational Chinese speech, but no progress. But in the written language, although the characters were inherited from former time, the technique of their formation was improved, and so were their finish and elegance. Hence

THE MISTAKE OF THE CHINESE SAGES

Chinese is the strangest and most awkward language in the world: often it used to be impossible to convey the meaning of a word otherwise than by writing. The Chinese are not bad writers; but very clumsy conversationalists. This can easily be explained. The art of writing could be handed down from the most remote ages. The old classics could easily be imitated. But while speech may be distinguished by the composition and polish of well-turned phrases, both in ordinary conversation and in oratory, these unfortunately cannot be conveyed for lack of recording, and thus in time they are lost. Hence arise the progress of writing and the regress of speech.

Moreover, in European languages the writing of words is founded upon vocal sounds, and books are written in the customary tongue: when the vocal sounds change, so does the language, and the written language changes accordingly. Things are otherwise in Chinese. In the Chinese language the mode of writing words is based on two principles. The first is that the character must bear a resemblance to the thing it represents: the second is that it must be composed in such a way that its meaning can be guessed from an analysis of its component parts. If the composition of the Chinese characters is so complicated, it is not surprising that Chinese writing has not been influenced by the changes in speech.

The compositions of gifted writers in Chinese

63

history excel those of foreign writers—this is universally recognised. As Chinese writing is itself an art, and gifted writers are in their way artists, thanks to their painstakingly polished works, knowledge of Chinese literature cannot be acquired by an average mind. Of course we may condemn the evil, which has spread to an unexpected extent, that all have concentrated on one form of art—the study of literature—and have neglected all others.

There are many first-class writers in the history of Chinese literature; but still I ask our Chinese writers, did they know all the rules of Chinese writing before they began their literary career? The reply will be "No." We have no grammar. Persons who study Chinese writing often begin by devoting themselves to the study of the characters, and only gradually achieve the understanding of the modes of writing: their style unconsciously adapts itself to the rules of grammar. It would be difficult to find writers whose works could be analysed with a view to determining " what ought to have been " the distribution of words and phrases, and " why " each word was used. When they are asked about their mode of thought, they justify themselves by saying that every man must learn and develop independently, and no established rules or methods can be given you. This reply shows how poorly informed our scholars are. The Chinese respect scholars as persons who study the meaning of " what ought to be " and " why it should be." If they only know that one must act in a certain way, but cannot explain it, they cannot be respected as scholars.

When we desire to know " what ought to be " in literary works, we must begin the study of the rules of language. When we desire to know " why it should be " we must study the science of reflection. The study of the rules of language in the Western countries is called " grammar." It teaches us to analyse phrases, to divide words amongst different parts of speech, to make the syntax of a phrase which has been composed : all in order that you should express your thought correctly. Every country in the West has its grammar, built up appropriately to its language. It is an elementary study for beginners. Hence, by the time children are ten years old, they usually know their grammar already, and can deal with the words which they require for writing compositions. In this way, notwithstanding the differing attainments in knowledge of different pupils, older or younger, none of them will write incorrectly when composing a literary exercise, and it will rarely happen that they use a word wrongly.

But in China up to this day there is no such thing as grammar. Those who learn to write, unless they keep to the repetition or paraphrase of model or classical examples, in order, by this means to learn style, cannot write Chinese correctly. Therefore those who are already working at their subject very earnestly, and have acquired a grasp of it, can write well. Whereas those who don't know how to begin this study will never achieve any result even if they rake over the bookshops for a dozen years together, and will continue to write Chinese incorrectly just the same.

If we give our children ten characters to learn a day, and explain their meaning to them, they will know three thousand characters in a year ; but if you ask them to write the simplest composition out of these characters, they will not be able to do it. As they don't know grammar, and therefore cannot find the shortest way to write a thing correctly, they have to grope their way in the dark for several years. It is just the same as crossing a stream. If there is no bridge or boat handy, a traveller must go a long way round before he finds the way to cross to the other side. Truly unhappy is the lot of the Chinese.

From the moment of the appearance of the book entitled *Chinese Grammar,* China for the first time became possessed of this branch of knowledge. The author of this book spent tens of years in research and study when composing it. But if we examine more closely the significance of this book, we shall see that it contains only the proof that the writings of the classics unconsciously coincide with the rules of grammar, and a confirmation of the necessity of grammar for Chinese writers in order to improve their work. Although it may be used as a reference book by skilled writers, it cannot serve as a text-book for beginners.

Since the great work of Mr. Ma, many books on the same subject have been printed. But although they are considered helpful for beginners, it is nevertheless regrettable that their authors were not acquainted with the secrets of the Chinese language, and consequently they contain some mistakes and vulgar turns of speech. Moreover, to illustrate the principles which they establish they quote exclusively the ancient writings, making no use of modern speech, and therefore these works cannot be understood by persons little acquainted with classical literature. While the man who has already mastered the Chinese language does not require them : he has already discovered the ford whereby to cross the river, and he does not need to seek a bridge.

We value bridges so long as we have not crossed the river : in the same way children ten years of age, who don't know how to write, need help in order to learn. I sincerely hope that the great Chinese scholars will occupy themselves with studying the grammatical systems of various countries on a large scale, and then with adapting their rules to the Chinese language, as its improvement undoubtedly demands. If there is a Chinese grammar, and the Chinese people is made acquainted with it, and will know it sufficiently to use proper expressions, they will be able, thanks to this grammar, to understand the ancient writings, and then it will be as easy to write Chinese well as to turn a hand. Then uniformity between written and conversational speech can be re-established.

What is the science of writing reflections? In the Western countries it is called logic. The author uses the expression: " the science of writing reflections " to translate the word " logic " not because it is the most suitable, but because he thinks that logic applied to writing is reflection. Modern writers usually apply this science in order to draw correct conclusions, and therefore some translate the word as " the science of reflection," while others translate it as " the science of argumentation." Of course, these are by no means the most exact translations. The science of correct deduction embraces only one part of logic, while argumentation is only one part of deduction, and its scope is very limited. Of course, the expressions do not cover the whole of logic, and cannot convey its exact translation.

Those who translate the term " logic " as " the science of reflection " or " the science of argumentation " see only a part of the truth. It is just the same as the Chinese who live in foreign parts calling Spain Manilla. This is an historical error. Manilla is an island in Oceania, near China. Thousands of year ago Chinese navigators often visited these places, and therefore the Chinese became accustomed to the name. Later on, Manilla was occupied by Spain. Since that time, the Chinese who visited Manilla called the Spaniards Manillans. Later on, when they visited the United States of America, Mexico, Chile and Peru, and saw the Spaniards there dominating various territories, they began to call these Spaniards also Manillans. Later still, when they learned that the so-called " Manillans " have their own country, they began calling Spain " Great Manilla " and the island " Little Manilla." So it has remained to this day. From the point of view of scientific accuracy we can only speak of " Spain," including in it Manilla, but cannot speak of " Manilla " and include Spain in the term. But the Chinese abroad know no other Spain than " Manilla," and continue to use that name, side by side with the real name. Chinese logicians who translate " logic " by the name of its part are similar to these Chinese abroad.

But what is logic, and how is this word best rendered ? The author would like to consider this question. Those who are familiar with logic know that it is the science of all the sciences, opening the way to correct thinking and correct acts. There is a vast number of people who unconsciously think logically, although they never studied logic. In China this science has no name. In the opinion of the author, its name must be translated as " li-chieh." This branch of learning has not yet been fully developed. Those who devote themselves to it cannot be of the same opinion about it. There are very many conflicting opinions. Those

who do not devote themselves to the science are
indifferent to it, as the power of logical reflection
is amongst man's inborn qualities. When skilful
writers are plunged in deep meditation and
produce immortal works, they do this unconsciously. If we ask them, by what paths they
reached these heights, they cannot tell us. Furthermore, they are quite ignorant of the paths by which
they moved. Not knowing grammar, they do not
even know " that which should have been."

Let me quote an example to make my point
clear. Mr. Chen-Kuo-Fan was, as we know, the
greatest scholar at the time of the fall of the
Ching dynasty. When he was discussing literary
productions with others, he quoted well-known
ancient expressions, such as : " the spring breezes
blow, the summer rains rain," " untie the clothes
to clothe me," " give me food to feed me," to
prove that similar words " breezes—blow," " rains
—rain," " clothes—clothe," " food—feed," are
used here in different senses. He said that the
first words were nouns proper, while the second were
" nouns used virtually." Mr. Chen considered
this a discovery without precedent, and, having
given this explanation, he considered that he had
found the key to the secrets locked up in ancient
manuscripts. But from the grammatical point
of view the first words are nouns, the second are
verbs, and this seems very simple. But the most
gifted writer of olden times did not know this,
and explained verbs as " nouns, used virtually."

THE MISTAKE OF THE CHINESE SAGES

Those who are ignorant of logic do not know also the purpose (" what for ") of Chinese writings. In a recent work entitled, *A Short Sketch of Chinese Grammar*, the third chapter contains the following passage : " Proper names serve only to designate persons and things. Thus, Mr. F. I. How, in his sketch of Wang-Heng, Chancellor during the Chin dynasty, said : ' Just as, about 2000 years ago, Chin-Kuo-Liang was loyal and honest to the end towards the Han dynasty, so was Wang-Heng towards the Chin dynasty.' Mr. Kung-Chi-Kuei, in his *Appeal to the Northern Mountains*, writes : ' There is emptiness behind the splendid curtains, the nightingale complains, man has gone to the hills, the ape is astonished.' In the examples given, although Chin-Kuo-Liang and Wang-Heng are human beings, while the nightingale and the ape belong to the animal world, all four nouns are proper names, because not all human beings are called Chin-Kuo-Liang or Wang-Heng, not every animal is a bird or ape. Such nouns are called proper names." In this example the writer of the book referred to, considers Chin-Kuo-Liang, Wang-Heng, the nightingale, the ape, as names of the same type. This, of course, is quite wrong, not only in the eyes of one who runs through a text-book, but even for an uneducated man who can reflect logically.

But why did the writer make this mistake ? Because in China there is no such science as logic, while men rarely make use of the power of logical thinking born in them.

Chinese authors are talented and numerous, their works are excellent and elegant. That which they write can inspire heaven and earth, as Mr. Yuan-Hsiung once said. But for several thousands of years the Chinese have been able only to write, not to know how they write. The Chinese have had no one to invent grammar or logic before foreigners introduced these sciences into our country. Is not this an example of the fact that " actions are easy, but knowledge difficult ?"

CHAPTER II

" TO UNDERSTAND IS DIFFICULT, BUT TO ACHIEVE IS EASY "

(*Seven More Proofs*)

IT seems to me that the theory of the easiness of action and the difficulty of understanding might be considered sufficiently proved by the three examples already given. But it is said that this may be true, yet nevertheless this leaves a gap which has to be filled, in that other cases might be different.

Therefore I shall try to prove the correctness of my theory by seven more examples, namely, the building of houses, shipbuilding, the building of fortifications, the digging of canals, electricity, chemistry and evolution, and we shall see whether the theory is true in all these cases.

The science of architecture only appeared a thousand years after mankind began building themselves dwellings with many comforts. China up to this day has no architecture. Chinese houses are not built according to the plans of architectural science. It is quite otherwise with foreign buildings. All of them are founded on architectural science. First a sketch is made,

73

then a plan is worked out, and only then do they begin construction. This is action carried out in the first place by knowledge. The plans of buildings in Shanghai are worked out by foreign architects, while the work of building is carried out by Chinese coolies. In this case the men who possess knowledge are the foreign architects, while the men who assume the labour of completing the buildings are the Chinese workers. The structure is completed by the efforts and co-operation of knowledge and action.

If we look at things superficially, it will appear to us that the architects have taken on the lighter work, because they work only with their pen : But if we consider the matter more closely, we shall realise the vast difference between the difficulty of the plan and the easiness of the work—as far apart as heaven and earth.

Imagine that a man wishes to build a house costing ten thousand dollars. He goes first of all to an architect and asks him to draw up a plan, and questions him about the capacity of the house and the materials required. The architect who undertakes the work has to calculate the various materials which will have to be procured, and their various qualities, without going beyond the bounds of ten thousand dollars. This is a problem of practical economy. Secondly, the architect has to reckon out the area of the land on which the house is to stand, to calculate its capacity in cubic yards, the pressure of the building, the weight which the foundations or piles can bear. All this the architect must reckon out accurately, and all this involves a knowledge of applied physics. Further, how should the house be built : fashionably, comfortably or handsomely ? This is drawn from practical æsthetics. Then knowledge of how the sun's rays should be absorbed, how the air is to move freely through the building, how the house is to be protected against cold and heat, how dirt and rubbish is to be disposed of—this comes from the sphere of domestic sanitation. Lastly, the architect must know how the drawing-room should be fitted, how the study should be equipped, how the rooms should be made cosy and comfortable— this comes from the sphere of social psychology. The architect has to draw his plans, relying on information drawn from the branches of knowledge mentioned, if he desires to become famous.

Lofty buildings of several stories and private houses of foreigners in Shanghai are built according to the plans of very skilful architects. But they were built by Chinese coolies. If we are to judge from this example, which is the easier, knowledge or action ? Thus architecture may serve as the fourth proof of the correctness of the theory that action is easy but knowledge difficult.

In October of the 7th year of our Republic (1918) a Chinese shipyard at Shanghai built a ship of three thousand tons. When it was launched the foreign Press loudly welcomed the fact. The

Press said that this was the largest ship ever built in China, and worthy of notice. Yet the ship was built after the pattern of the ships of Western countries ; it involved the application of knowledge of modern sciences and of foreign machines. It is said that of late all the workmen in the foreign shipyards at Shanghai, Hong Kong and the islands of Oceania have been Chinese. Only a few engineers and the directors come from a foreign race. To-day there are already many ships with a displacement of over ten thousand tons, built in such yards. In a word, we can say without exaggeration, that in the East, in the foreign shipyards, the ships have all been built by Chinese, because the contracts for building go through the hands of Chinese.

The author has visited several shipyards to become acquainted with the works. When questioning Chinese workmen about the technique of shipbuilding, I observed that the process of construction is not at all difficult, but the difficulty lies in the drawing of plans and sketches. If the latter have been completed, the structural work will proceed according to them and will be soon completed.

Last year (1917), when the United States declared war on Germany, the most powerful armament, which had to be procured at all costs, was the construction of a fleet. America had to take unheard-of steps to increase its shipbuilding works. A year was given as the time for building

76

ships with a total to average of 4,000,000 tons.
When this plan was published by America, the
whole world grew anxious. If such a plan had
been proposed in normal times, the world would
have looked on it as a frantic and ridiculous
proposal. But America worked intensively. The
shipyards were able to complete ships of over
10,000 tons in a few weeks. There were over a
hundred shipyards in America. The large yards
undertook to build dozens of ships: the small
yards took a smaller quantity. They began work
simultaneously, and carried it on so intensively
that by the appointed time they had completed
the whole programme.

Recently a Japanese shipyard built a vessel of
10,000 tons in twenty-three days. This was a
world's record. But such a feat is the outcome
of modern science. Basing itself on knowledge,
mankind discusses plans before setting about their
fulfilment. The fulfilment of these plans is
extraordinary and amazing. It is worth com-
paring with the difficulties of shipbuilding before
the application of modern science. By this
comparison we can most vividly convince ourselves
of the truth of the theory that " action is easy,
but knowledge difficult."

At the beginning of the Ming dynasty (1398)
the Emperor Chen-Chu seven times sent his
eunuch, Chien-Ho, on a naval expedition to
discover and arrest the abdicated Emperor Chien-
Wen. The first time the eunuch sailed was in the

sixth month of the third lunar year of Tuien-Lo. He returned in the ninth month of the fifth lunar year of the same Emperor. During these months he visited all the islands of the ocean and even reached San Francisco. When we calculate the length of his journey and the time during which he was delayed on the way, we see that his journey could not have been completed in less than twenty-eight months. Let us divide twenty-eight months into two parts : the first the period of preparation, the second that of the journey. Let us assume that the first period took at least fourteen months. During this space of time, from the day he received the order to the day he sailed, Chien-Ho had to lay in stores for 28,000 men, arms for them, and all else that they required.

But most difficult of all was to procure sixty-four large ships, capable of taking the sea. This was a gigantic piece of work. According to the chroniclers of the Ming dynasty, all ocean-going ships were 440 feet long and 180 feet broad. Although we don't know how deep they were in the water, we can presume that 10 feet were below the water level. Therefore, the total number of tons might be 4000 to 5000. If we imagine the conditions of those times, we shall be able to appraise at its true value this remarkable piece of work. There was no scientific knowledge at that time, such as there is now to facilitate such work : there were no machines to replace handi-craft. Moreover, Chien-Ho was not a shipbuilder.

There were not even any ships of such a size before that day. But Chien-Ho was able in fourteen months to build sixty-four ocean-going ships, capable of holding 28,000 men, on which he sailed round all the islands of the ocean, in order to show abroad the awe-inspiring power of China, and caused the barbarous tribes there to remember the great deeds of Chien-Ho and admire the Chinese to the present day. It was indeed a very great achievement. If to-day the Chinese are able to build ships of 3000 tons with the help of modern science and foreign machinery, and this merits great praise, what is it in comparison with one ship built by Chien-Ho? Thus shipbuilding, as a fifth example, also confirms our theory.

The best-known architectural achievement in China is the so-called Great Wall. The Emperor Shih-Huang-Ti, of the Ching dynasty (240 B.C.) ordered his general Mong-Tieng to build a wall which could withstand the attacks of the Tartars. This great work began at Mukden in the East and ended in Shansi. It crossed mountains and valleys for a distance of 5000 li. There were no such works in ancient times: it was the wonder of the world. After all, in the days of the Ching dynasty, science was as yet unknown, machines did not exist, hand labour was not yet very varied, raw materials were not yet abundant, and the science of architecture was still in its embryo stage, and not so diversified as at present. How could the Chinese achieve such a success?

It is said that the Chinese did this, driven by necessity. The Western sayings have it that necessity is the mother of all inventions. Although this emperor of the Ching dynasty had with heroic courage conquered the whole of China, which was at that time divided into six small states, he was unable to cross the desert in order to crush the Tartars. To organise regular troops to repel unexpected attacks was difficult and onerous. Therefore for those times and succeeding years it was more suitable to erect a great wall, making it impregnable against the Tartars. Although the Emperor Shih-Huang-Ti was cruel and pitiless to his subordinates, his building of the Wall rendered humanity as great a service as that of the Great Yu, who rescued us from the Deluge. Now we can see and conceive that, if we had not been protected by the Great Wall, we should have been crushed by the Tartars. Our race would have been completely destroyed at the beginning of the Han dynasty (206 B.C. to 220 A.D.) If there had been no wall, the Chinese people would not have flourished later on: it would not have been so strong in the Han-Tong dynasties, and would not have been able to unite with itself the southern peoples of China.

The Chinese people reached maturity, developing physically and mentally at the same time, under the protection of the Great Wall, and although China later on fell a victim to the Mongol invasion, still the Mongols mingled with us and were amalgamated, and not the reverse, as sometimes may be observed in the history of nations.

Although later on the Chinese were subjugated by the Manchus, the latter could not escape the same fate as the Mongols. But before this strength of the Chinese people had developed and become consolidated, the Great Chinese Wall played its part, defending our people from invasion and enslavement by the barbarian tribes of the northern Tartars. The emperor thought by the building of this wall to strengthen the power of his descendants, and make it unshakable for ever, by protecting China from the Tartar invasion. He was not aware, and did not even dream, that, in defending our young and as yet immature Chinese civilisation from destruction at the hands of the northern Tartars, his Wall would produce such vast results. Necessity forced him to build the Wall at all costs, risking all else, and he paid no attention at all to the vast labour which it involved and the vast efforts which he had to expend on its construction. Historians also say that he achieved this without knowing beforehand how he would carry out his intention.

In our days of the supremacy of science and the perfection of machinery, human powers and the powers of machinery have surpassed the possibilities of the past, and the science of architecture has gone forward very rapidly. And if to-day we go to a skilled civil engineer and ask him to draw up the plan for the construction of a Great

F   81

Wall, to reckon up what quantity of materials it will require, how much time will be needed to complete the work, what sum is necessary for this purpose and how much labour will have to be expended, I think he will reply : " This is very difficult to ascertain." But if an engineer be found who will not quail before the task, and who makes a detailed calculation involving several years of work, calculates everything, draws up a plan, and submits it to the judgment of the people, the latter will scarcely say that the execution (action) is difficult, while the knowledge is easy.

Let me give another object-lesson. I will ask my readers to recall the battle-fields of Europe during the Great War. When the attempt of the German troops to seize Paris failed for the first time, and they were forced to pass from the offensive to the defensive, the army dug a very long trench, beginning from the shores of the North Sea and ending at the foot of the Swiss mountains, in a few weeks. Its length is estimated to have been 1500 miles. It contained three lines of fortifications. In every line there were underground trenches, earthworks, fortified communication trenches and storehouses. So far as the complexity and impregnability of this work is concerned, one mile of it in every line meant more than all the work expended on the Great Chinese Wall. The total length of these three lines was not less than 5000 miles. The same length of trenches was dug on the side of the Entente, in order to be able to resist the Germans. Thus the length of this work on both sides amounted to 10,000 miles, i.e. twice the length of the Great Wall.

These trenches were not thought out before-hand : they were constructed as a matter of urgency. But the magnitude of the undertaking and the rapidity of its completion are to some extent, one might say, a secret. Yet, this is not all. The line of military operations in Eastern Europe, stretching from the Baltic Sea across the whole continent to the Black Sea, was three times longer than the western battlefield. The opposing forces faced one another in trenches of the same length, just as happened in Western Europe. The time required for this work was the same. Such a gigantic enterprise might have seemed to us impossible to carry out, if these trenches had not been a fact. But the battle-fields both in Western and Eastern Europe have now become a matter of history : there are no traces left. Even military engineering experts would discover them with difficulty : yet they are a fact. Thus from all the above it is clear that our Chinese Great Wall and the great European battlefields may serve as a sixth proof of the theory about the easiness of action and the difficulty of knowledge.

There was still one more gigantic piece of work in China, second only to the Great Wall : this was the Imperial Grand Canal. It began at Hangchow and crossed the provinces of Kiangsu, Shantung and Chihli. It was crossed by the Yangtze-kiang, the Yellow River, the White River, and ended at Tengchow, in the north. Its length is 1000 miles: it was the first and longest canal in the world. It served as an important means of internal communication by water between Southern and Northern China, bringing innumerable advantages to our country and our people. After China entered into trading relations with foreign countries, steamship communication began to be utilised on a large scale. Maritime intercourse developed, and the Canal began to fall into disuse. It began to be silted up, and in many places it is almost completely blocked and threatens to overflow.

Of late there have been many people who suggested lowering the level of the Canal at various points between the Yangtze River and the River Hwai, in order to bring it once again into use. Engineers who were invited to investigate the possibilities came to the conclusion that it would be no light task, and that the expenses would be so great as to render necessary consideration of floating a foreign loan to finance it. It stands to reason that the deepening of a canal is an easier piece of work than cutting it in the first place: the improvement of part of a river is easier than creating the whole river. But people to-day, before even beginning the working-out of

84

a plan, already realise the difficulties facing them, whereas people in olden days could brilliantly accomplish the digging of a canal 1000 miles long as though it were nothing out of the ordinary. Why is this so ? Because the real difficulty of the work arises, not in the period of its execution, but rather at the beginning, in the period of its discussion and planning. The people of olden times were not as learned as the people of to-day ; when they intended to do something, they did not put off their work for long conversations and discussions at the very beginning. They first set about the task in the way dictated by vital necessity. Their success and skill advanced together, but unconsciously. That is how matters stood when the Grand Canal was being built, i.e. the Chinese carried out this work without any preliminary plan.

There are many canals in the world. The most remarkable are the Suez and Panama Canals. The Suez Canal is at the end of the Mediterranean Sea and connects it with the Red Sea. It shortened communication between the Atlantic and Indian Oceans. From the most ancient times the intention to dig this canal has existed. In 1798, when Napoleon conquered Egypt, he determined to construct this canal between the two seas. He ordered an engineer to investigate the isthmus, with a view to preliminary operations. The engineer came to the conclusion that the difference in level between the Red and Mediterranean Seas comes to 29 feet, and Napoleon's plan was abandoned.

Only in the '50's of last century did some Frenchmen again take it up, and discover that the previous calculations were inaccurate, and that the difference in levels was not so great. In 1854 Ferdinand de Lesseps began to agitate in favour of the idea of organising a company to construct a ship canal across the isthmus. He was made a subject for ridicule and jokes, particularly in England, where the whole people rejected the plan as quite impracticable, and thought it must inevitably end in failure. But de Lesseps applied all his energies to winning the approval of his own people, in spite of the stubborn resistance offered by the whole world to the plan he proposed. Finally, he succeeded in convincing the people, and, with the support of French capitalists and the Egyptian Viceroy, the Suez Canal Company was founded in 1858. The next year the work of construction began, and in 1869 the Suez Canal was officially opened.

Thereupon the British Prime Minister, Disraeli, began to try his hardest to acquire for the British Government the shares in the Suez Canal Company, which were held by the Egyptian Khedives. Later on he even added Egypt to the British possessions, on the plea that Great Britain must protect the Canal, in order to have control over the passage between the Mediterranean and Red Seas and maintain communication by sea with India.

"TO UNDERSTAND IS DIFFICULT . . ."

After his successful attempt to construct the Suez Canal, de Lesseps became a world-famous and universally respected man. He then began to devote much attention to the plan of digging the Panama Canal, in order to provide the possibility of communication between the Atlantic and Pacific Oceans. Very soon application forms for shares began to be filled up, and they were taken up immediately. Construction began in 1882 : in 1889 the Company went completely bankrupt, and de Lesseps was also punished. There were two reasons for the bankruptcy : first, lack of funds, and secondly, the epidemic of malaria which prevailed there. The epidemic carried off too many people on the undertaking, and on account of this it could not continue.

The lack of money could, of course, be remedied, but matters were much worse with the epidemic. If it continued, it would scarcely be possible to continue. Science at that time was not able to cope with the problem of making the Isthmus of Panama healthy. Therefore work was temporarily suspended. However, modern science later on established that all diseases come from bacteria, and the epidemic at Panama, i.e. malaria, was disseminated by insects (mosquitoes). When the Government of the United States decided to continue the construction of the Panama Canal, it first of all undertook the work of destroying the insects. and took a number of other steps to make the district more healthy. When this had been done, construction was resumed, and was successfully completed in 1918. And from that time communication between the Altantic and Pacific Oceans became an actual fact.

Hence we see that the chief reason for de Lesseps' failure lay in his ignorance of the destructive activities of insects, while the reason for the success of the United States Government was entirely that, anticipating the peril of sickness due to these insects, it took measures to destroy them. Thus this case is one of the proofs of my theory.

For a long time China has been proud of being the first country to invent ship's instruments. Many other things invented by China have greatly assisted the development of world civilisation. Amongst these must be classed printing, gunpowder, porcelain, silk and tea, all of which mankind requires. But there is yet one thing more, which assisted in the growth of world relations and a closer connection between the peoples. This was the Chinese compass. Historians say that the compass was invented by the Emperor Hwangti (a legendary monarch, in 2698 B.C.), but others assert that it was discovered by Choe-Kung, a duke and prime minister at the beginning of the Chow dynasty (1125-255 B.C.) However, leaving aside the question of the name of the inventor of the compass, it was undoubtedly the Chinese who long ago discovered the nature of the magnet and invented the compass. Later the Western countries applied it to ocean-travelling, which assisted in the development of maritime communication.

If there were no compass to indicate direction, it is unlikely that anyone would venture to set sail on a distant and boundless sea. If there were no compass, maritime exploration would not have developed, and civilisation would not have reached its present level. Thus the benefits conferred by the compass are enormous. But what is the compass ? It is a simple electrical machine. Men began to make use of electricity when they utilised the compass. From the time that the compass came into use, mankind began to study the principles according to which the pointer of the compass is always directed at one end to the south, at the other to the north. Why does the magnet attract iron ? Only after thousands of years of effort and research did mankind discover electricity. It discovered that electricity is not material, that its essence can be transformed into heat and light. It penetrates everywhere and permeates the whole of the atmosphere. When it passes along the earth, it has a definite direction, from south to north. When the magnet is under the influence of electricity, it has the tendency to point north and south, just as a weathercock under the influence of the wind turns in the direction in which the wind is moving.

Formerly, when human knowledge of electricity was still small, mankind looked on lightning and thunder as gods, and worshipped them ; now it uses them for its domestic requirements. To-day we call our age " the age of electricity." To-day mankind cannot do without electricity. If we look at towns and ports, we see that the consumption of electricity increases day by day. We light electric lamps. We make use of electricity in travelling, we can talk with the help of electricity, we can communicate with one another by means of electricity, we work with electricity, we cure sicknesses with the help of electricity, we prepare food on electricity, we utilise it for heating, etc. But I ask : many people use electricity, but how many of them know what it is ?

When a new invention appears, for example the dynamo, the world gradually becomes accustomed to utilise this invention. For example, the great invention of recent times, the wireless telegraph, which in the space of a few years has spread all over the world. Yet this discovery swallowed up centuries of effort, exhausted the knowledge of many scientists, for everyone of them gave his portion of knowledge, before the conception of wireless telegraphy was fully grasped. Relying on scientific truth and exact knowledge, of course, it is not very difficult to invent machines. To-day everyone can carry on their correspondence by wireless telegraphy. Everyone can also occupy the post of an operator in a wireless telegraph station. The mechanics who manufacture wireless telegraph apparatus are not faced any longer with a difficult task. The heaviest burden lies on the backs of scientists, and, once this difficulty is overcome, all the rest goes well. From the application of electricity we learn that when mankind still did not know of electricity it already had the magnet and utilised it for the compass to assist navigation. Thus electricity constitutes the eighth proof of the theory that action is easy and knowledge difficult.

The development of modern science is secured not by the progress of any special branch of knowledge, but rather by the united efforts of various sciences and their mutual assistance in this striving forward. One branch of science which approaches closest of all to electricity is chemistry.

If chemistry makes no progress, electricity also can hardly go forward alone. And, vice versa, the progress of chemistry is possible only on condition of new inventions in the sphere of electricity. The forerunner of chemistry is Taoistic alchemy. In ancient times people sought for the elixir of life by all possible means, in the hope of achieving their goal. Although the elixir was not discovered, these experiments stimulated the development of chemistry. The most outstanding discoveries of chemistry in China, are the production of vitriol, gunpowder, porcelain and bean oil. In China this chemical production has existed for several thousands of years, but the Chinese only continued on the old track in this sphere, not knowing the inner significance, or even that such a mode of production is called chemistry.

At present modern Chinese scientists have an uncommon yearning after Western sciences, and the most wonder-working branch of learning which interests them is chemistry. The most difficult part of chemistry to study is organic chemistry, the most important part of which is that which treats of foodstuffs. Western physiologists in recent times have by means of experiment arrived at the conclusion that in animal (meat) food there are many harmful substances. But here another problem arises : that which man chiefly requires for his sustenance is contained chiefly in meat. If we cease to eat meat and seek equivalent nutritive matter elsewhere, shall we find any means of achieving this ? This is why the question of the hygiene of diet is an old problem, which scientists try very hard to solve.

Of late, biology has developed very quickly. Many great discoveries have been made by French chemists. They created organic chemistry. Making use of the method of synthesis to procure organic material, they have even set before themselves the aim of preparing foodstuffs by means of chemistry. M. Pasteur founded bacteriology, by which he facilitated the appearance of biochemistry. His followers have applied biochemistry to the study of foodstuffs, and have thus come to the conclusion that meat contains poisonous substances and that vegetables are the best food.

My friend Mr. Li-Shi-Chen, who was educated in France, a pupil of Pasteur, has studied agriculture and paid great attention to beans. He founded the " International Society for the Preparation of Bean Milk," and affirmed that bean milk can entirely replace cow's milk, and bean foods, meat. He based his conclusions on the theories of many chemists and on experiments in the use of vegetarian food. He also founded the " Bean Milk Society." Of course, the Chinese have been eating bean mash from very far-off times ; and, needless to say, many of them know how to prepare it. Even in very remote villages with a small population there are factories of bean extract. We despised this food as the most common. But, by a strange irony of fate, it turned out to be one of the most wonderful products of organic chemistry, the most economical and beneficial food. Furthermore, it is that same valuable food which the most renowned scientists of to-day are trying, and failing, to discover.

Let me quote another example : the manufacture of pottery. It has been going on almost from prehistoric times. In Babylon and Egypt people used clay tablets to make books, and manufactured bricks of clay before the Western people discovered this building material. All the ancestors of the civilised peoples of to-day made earthenware independently. We see that, by baking clay, we

93

can produce pottery, and this can be done by any nation which has reached the age of fire. But the manufacture of porcelain is the particular original invention of China. Up to this day Chinese porcelain is considered the most perfect of its kind. In 1540 a certain Frenchman, B., saw Chinese porcelain in an aristocratic family. He judged it to be the most precious of objects, and determined to imitate the method of its manufacture, in order that the common people might also enjoy the use of this valuable discovery. He studied the technique of its manufacture for sixteen years, and then built a kind of pottery workshop. This was the beginning of the imitation by Europeans of the Chinese method of manufacturing porcelain.

In recent times chemistry in the Western countries has developed to an extraordinary degree, and is bringing with it industrial development. The manufacture of porcelain is also based on a knowledge of chemistry, and its production in the West at the present time almost reaches the standard attained by Chinese porcelain. But if it be compared with the artistic porcelain produced in the time of Woen-Lo-Ching-Tai, of the Ming dynasty, and of Kiat-Hsi and Chien-Lung of the Ching dynasty, its colours and quality will be discovered to be much lower than those of Chinese productions, which are positively unequalled.

The development of chemistry to-day has reached the widest bounds, and the marvels it

94

works, of course, have far outstripped the wonders of alchemy in the past. Previously there existed a difference between organic and inorganic chemistry, but now there can be no more distinctions, since the advancing technique of chemistry may transform inorganic chemistry into organic. Moreover, the so-called theory of elements and atoms has also been destroyed, as the discovery of radium breaks down the atomic theory and demonstrates the incorrectness of the assertion that atoms and elements are indivisible ; on the contrary, these atoms consist of still smaller units, called electrons. Thus from now onwards a new era is opening in chemistry.

The Western peoples, imitating the Chinese in the manufacture of porcelain, founded their work on the analysis of substances. So far as the quality and colouring of porcelain are concerned they have been chemically studied most carefully ; but the technique of the firing of porcelain belongs exclusively to the sphere of human talent. This kind of technique has ceased to extend, and its development was arrested, as a result of which it is no longer possible to imitate it. This is why Europeans most of all admire porcelain of the Ming and Ching dynasties, and very often do not grudge thousands of dollars to acquire it. All that they can collect in their museums is considered to be one of the rarest works of art. But the Chinese craftsmen who made this kind of porcelain were ignorant of chemistry and physics.

Thus chemistry is the ninth confirmation of my theory.

Let us now consider the theory of evolution. Its discovery was the work of Darwin, who wrote a great book: *The Origin of Species*. Since that time the world has known that all species are obliged to evolution for their existence. The most learned philosophers of ancient and modern times, who studied the origin of species, could not prove this conclusion. Two thousand years ago the Greek philosopher, Democritus, had realised that all creatures come by the path of evolution. But he had no followers, and the theory of evolution did not receive a foundation. During the European Renaissance, freedom of thinking again reigned, and the philosopher Spinoza studied the world from its external aspect, declaring as a result in favour of the theory of evolution. Spinoza was the spiritual father and inspiration of Darwin. Later on, after the Renaissance, the development of science went ahead rapidly. Many discoveries were made at that time. The most remarkable discoveries were those of Laplace in the realm of astronomy, Lyell in that of geology, and Lamarck in that of zoology. All these great men, by means of the conclusions drawn by them from science, arrived at the theory of evolution and may be called its pioneers.

Darwin studied it by means of the observation of animals. After twenty years of research he published his book *The Origin of Species*, to

explain the theory of natural selection and the
struggle for existence. With the publication of
this book, the theory of evolution produced a
complete change in science. Thoughts and ideals
were sharply changed, and came under the
influence of this new philosophy. Since then all
sciences have based themselves on this theory.
The theory of evolution is the natural explanation
of the world-wide progress of all creatures. The
mutual struggle for existence, natural selection,
and the survival of the fittest are the principal
rules of the evolution of species. These principles
have been applied from the Stone Age onwards,
for the improvement of the seeds of plants. By
this means mankind has changed wild grasses
into cultivated plants, and has transformed wild
beasts into domestic animals. Men applied this
theory in practice for thousand of years, without
comprehending its significance. Only in the age of
scientific enlightenment was Darwin able at last
to conceive it, after working at the problem
unremittingly for twenty years.

From this we can judge of the difficulty of
knowledge. Darwin's discovery was compared
with Isaac Newton's discovery of the law of
gravity. Men considered these the two greatest
discoveries : the first in the sphere of time, the
second in the sphere of space. The writer considers
that there are three degrees or periods of evolution :
the first of matter, the second of species, and the
third of man. During the period of vapour, the

ether brought electrons into motion, the electrons produced matter and matter produced the earth.

This was the first stage of world evolution. But there are other heavenly bodies which are still in this stage of evolution. The evolution of matter is directed towards the formation of earth. How many million years were required for the formation of our planet? According to calculations based on the study of geological phenomena, twenty million years have passed since the time of the formation of the earth.

The period from the origin of cells to the appearance of man constitutes the second period of evolution. All species, from the smallest to the largest, from the simplest to the most complicated, according to the laws of the struggle for existence, natural selection, and the survival of the fittest, were already in existence when man appeared on the earth. Thousands of years passed before mankind acquired human nature, since in the first period of its existence it was in no way distinguishable from animals. Then began the evolution of mankind.

The foundations of the evolution of mankind were quite different from the basic principles of the evolution of other creatures. Amongst the latter the struggle for existence was the law, whereas men were guided by the principle of mutual aid. Society and the sciences are the concrete expression of this mutual aid. Morality, love, friendship and justice—all these are forms of expressing mutual aid. Mankind develops and progresses only on the condition that it obeys these fundamental laws, otherwise it perishes. The fact that mankind has still not applied these laws in practice on a large scale, and some people infringe them, arises from man's evolution from the animals, and from the fact that the third stage, into which man is entering as "man," is still very short. The animal heritage, or "instinct," has not yet been extinguished, and has not completely disappeared.

But once mankind entered the period of civilisation, his inner being spontaneously sought the principles of mutual aid, and was able to achieve the fundamental aim of human evolution. What is the end of human evolution? It is the aim indicated by Confucius when he said: "When your goal has been reached, you can live on the earth as in the heavens." These are the hopes of mankind, which desires to transform the present painful period of its existence into a happy paradise on earth. Modern civilisation is moving forward with gigantic strides, the progress of the last century may be compared with the progress of the last thousands of years, and as in the future the development of the last ten years will be comparable with the road travelled in the last hundred years, we can calculate the rapidity of progress and realise that the times we dream of are not far away. From the time that Darwin discovered the principles of evolution—the struggle for life of animals, natural selection, the survival of the fittest—scientists began to treat morality, love, justice and friendship as a mirage, and to regard the law of the struggle for existence as the reality. They even want to apply these laws of the animal world to mankind, but they do not understand that that only applied to a transitional period in the history of mankind—that the evolution of man has outgrown this principle which governs the world of animals. Thus the theory of evolution may serve as a tenth proof of my theory concerning the easiness of knowledge and the difficulty of action.

If the reader still does not believe my words, I ask him to notice the words of Confucius: " If the people are capable of action, let them proceed along its path ; but if not, then make them first of all understand this truth." From this saying we can see that the ancient sage also foreshadowed my theory.

CHAPTER III

THE CHINESE NEED KNOWLEDGE AND REVOLUTIONARY ACTION

AS the ten proofs of the theory of " the easiness of action and the difficulty of knowledge," set forth in the previous chapters, are sufficient to show the truth of that theory, the traditional Chinese phrase : " knowledge is easy but action is difficult," and the teaching of Wang-Yuan-Ming about " the unity in action of knowledge and deeds," must lose their hold over the human mind. Perhaps many of my readers think that these proofs can be applied only to material factors. I want to take advantage of this occasion to quote an extract from the " work of Meng-Sin " in the *Four Books,* to show that this doubt is unnecessary. There it is said : " To act without consideration, to act according to custom, without reflection, and to continue on one's path, throughout the whole of life, without understanding its purpose—this is the lot of the mob." Thus my theory, here also, finds confirmation, and consequently we can say that in all circumstances the theory is undoubtedly correct.

From a study of the works of Wang-Yuan-Ming, we may arrive at the conclusion that he knew very well the law of " the easiness of action and the difficulty of knowledge ; " but as his purpose was to concentrate the general attention more upon " action " (facts) than upon " knowledge," in order to make the Chinese people pay more attention to action than to speeches, he expressed his thought by speaking of the " functional unity of action and knowledge," and enlarged upon this theme to his pupils thus : " Do what you ought to do : for if you will not act thus, what value is there in your knowledge ? Your knowledge will lose its meaning, and worse still, that which you think you know will be quite unknown to you." Beyond all doubt, his idea of encouraging people to do good was very important, but still he made a mistake in taking the " difficult " for the " easy," and vice versa : and this brought him to a distortion of the truth. It is like making a man work at that which goes against human nature. Instead of starting with the habit of " acting without consideration, acting according to custom, without reflection, and continuing on their path, throughout the whole of life, without understanding its purpose," people become irresolute, and fall under the influence of the theory of Wang-Yuan-Ming. Thus it turns out that the teaching of Wang-Yuan-Ming is of little help to man, although it certainly exerted a great influence over the minds of Chinese scholars.

Perhaps someone will ask me : " Did not Japan derive benefit from the teaching of Wang-Yuan-Ming during the time of her reforms ? " To reply to this question it is necessary to become acquainted with Japanese history. Before the beginning of the reforms feudalism prevailed in Japan. But, in proportion as foreigners invaded Japan, and the feudal nobles were unable to prevent this invasion, there arose amongst the Japanese people a patriotic movement in favour of the expulsion of the " aliens," which was very similar to the watchwords of the Boxer movement. In different conditions of time and space, this patriotic reactionary movement in two neighbouring countries, Japan and China, produced quite different results.

After its first defeats in the attempt at resistance, Japan followed the example of the Western countries and adopted their method of government. At the same time we see that the success of Japan in her own transformation depended a great deal on the enterprising nature of the Japanese. They were ignorant of a great deal which they ought to have done, but they worked without noticing this, i.e. " acting without reflection, and continuing on their path, throughout the whole of life, without understanding its purpose."

However, if it be supposed that the teaching of Wang-Yuan-Ming favourably affected the transformation of Japan, the question arises, why then does it not save China from poverty and weakness, notwithstanding the fact that amongst the Chinese there are many disciples of Wang-Yuan-Ming ? The reply would be : "Most probably because the Chinese somehow are too fond of postponing hard work and trying to avoid it." Undoubtedly, the Chinese people suffers from this defect, but can this serve as the main reason why the teaching of Wang-Yuan-Ming loses its potency in China ?

The Japanese began to carry through their reforms without being acquainted with their meaning : while the Chinese are wont, before undertaking any affair, to ask themselves, do they know it thoroughly, and, if they arrive at a positive reply, will again be tortured by doubt as to whether they will be able to cope with it, and complete the work once it has begun. This, of course, is correct from the point of view of science ; and so China still sits lolling, as usual, on her couch. Why ? Because her sons are confused and deceived by the traditional phrase— "knowledge is easy but action is difficult." And therefore they dare not begin to work at reform, since they think that they have insufficient knowledge, while "action is difficult."

The majority of the reformers of Japan, probably, had no conception of the problems which stood before them, but the reforming of Japan proved a brilliant success, thanks to the enterprise of the Japanese. Things are otherwise with China : when the Chinese people feel the necessity of reform, they must first of all comprehend its full significance, and, if they are not able to do so during the course of their whole life, death will come before work at the application of reforms can begin. While, if they do become thoroughly acquainted with the significance of reform, they will not carry it into effect because " action is difficult." Thus the teaching of Wang-Yuan-Ming did not help, but could not hinder the enterprising Japanese in the application of reforms to their country : but it undoubtedly prevented the irresolute Chinese from doing this, and thereby unquestionably brought them harm.

Moreover, the teaching of Wang-Yuan-Ming is applicable only to a certain period of time and to certain work, but certainly cannot be applied in all circumstances. As modern science develops more and more every day, the contact between knowledge and action also becomes more and more remote. The modern division of labour makes it unnecessary for a man at one and the same time to possess knowledge and to execute definite tasks. The division of labour dictates the division of the functions of knowledge and execution. In such conditions how can the teaching of Wang-Yuan-Ming, which does not correspond to the modern data of the experimental sciences, rule over the minds of the Chinese ?

On the other hand, why is so much written in Chinese literature about this theory ? Because they see the salvation of China in the discovery of this theory. China has been poor and weak for over four centuries. The cause of this lies in the " easiness of knowledge and the difficulty of action." This theory reigned over the minds of the Chinese scholars, and they influenced the masses of the Chinese people. The mistaking of the " difficult " for the " easy," and of the " easy " for the " difficult " forces the irresolute Chinese to be afraid of making a wrong decision. Therefore the Chinese never secure good results from the work they begin. They put on one side the problems involved in carrying out their plan, and usually devote themselves to studying those problems. Many of them never reach their goal. As a result, when any Chinese, after 20 or 30 years of stubborn toil, does arrive at a certain knowledge of his subject, he can no longer apply it in practice, because " action is difficult."

Thus no work can be carried out by the acquisition of knowledge alone, and no work can come out of the absence of " knowledge." That is why China is falling lower and lower, drifting down-stream.

If we look back at the history of China, we shall find many traces of former greatness. The most remote times, those of the Tang and Yuan dynasties, were in their way the infancy of Chinese civilisation. The times of the Chow dynasty might be called the period of the maturity of Chinese civilisation. It was at that time that the political, economic and educational systems, literature and the arts attained in China the same development, roughly, as they have to-day in the modern Western countries. This was the Golden Age of Chinese civilisation. As the civilisation of the period of the Chow dynasty was at a high stage of development, we can say that from the primitive ages of China to the Chow dynasty was the first period of progress, while from the Chow dynasty to the present day was the second period of decay.

The laws of human evolution usually go forward, but there are times, as has happened in the history of China, when they take the backward path. Why is this so ? It seems to me that it follows from the traditional formula of the Chinese : " knowledge is easy, but action is difficult." The people of ancient times were very simple and unsophisticated : they worked without analysing, and thought little of the necessity of knowing the principles on which their work was founded. They were concerned chiefly with the results and consequences of their work. Thus they did not pay much attention to methods or labour processes by which any given thing was produced : they looked only to the result of their labour. Therefore they also never looked for what was difficult and what was easy : and this was the reason why the civilisation of the period of the Chow dynasty went far ahead, almost to the bounds of its possible development. This gives us the right to call this period " the period of performance (by action) without understanding (without analysis)."

With the growth of intellectual development, and the progress of thought and experience, the Chinese began to question and doubt. From the time of the Chow dynasty the Chinese began to ask themselves the questions " why ? " " how ? " and so forth. If any affair lay before them, they asked themselves whether they thoroughly understood it or not. Therefore I call this period one of " action with reflection." It was just at this time, and in application to this ideal, that arose the theory of " the easiness of knowledge and the difficulty of action." As the people of that time doubted in everything they did, it was easy to catch them with the phrase " action is difficult, knowledge easy ; " they forgot that their ancestors attained their knowledge thanks to their curious and courageous mind.

First the Chinese were in the stage of " action without understanding," then in the stage of " action with reflection," then " action after reflection," and finally " understanding before action." Very often people of ancient times could achieve only one field of knowledge after centuries and millenniums of stubborn toil. This knowledge they handed on to their descendants, and they, acquiring it without hard work, began to come to the conclusion that " knowledge is easy." As the idea of " understanding before action " went hand in hand with the formula " action is difficult, but knowledge is easy," people ceased to want to carry anything through in practice, and were more concerned with full knowledge beforehand. This gives us the key to the comprehension of why, after the Chow dynasty, a retrograde period in Chinese history began.

From the scientific point of view we see that the evolution of humanity may be divided in three periods: the first period (from prehistoric times to the first stage of civilisation) one of "action without understanding;" the second period (from the first stage of civilisation to its age of maturity) one of "understanding after action;" and the third period (after the discovery and development of science) of "understanding before action." Without knowing of these stages, and particularly in ignorance of the tradition that "action is difficult, but knowledge is easy," the European nations have happily passed through all three periods, have reached the highest stage of civilisation, and are now advancing without thinking of any obstacles.

Marco Polo, an Italian who occupied an official post under Genghis-Khan, of the Yunan dynasty, wrote a book about China when he left his post and returned to his native land. As soon as this book appeared in Europe, the Europeans were greatly amazed, and would not believe that there could exist in the world such a country as China. Some of the Europeans declared that China was a country invented by Marco Polo, as all the information about China of that day set down by him bore witness to the fact that China had gone much further ahead than the European countries, and even had a great deal of which they had not the least conception. It was roughly the same as the impression created on the Chinese twenty years ago by the book about Europe *Hsus-Shu-Chi*, written by Chang-Tah.

From the foregoing we see that European civilisation 600 years ago was very young in comparison with the civilisation of China. We shall see this still more vividly from the example of the reforms in Japan. Only fifty years have passed since the time of the reforms in Japan, and she has already become a country with excellently developed trade, industry and arts, with a well-trained army and fleet, a well-organised Government and educational, economic and political systems. Briefly, her civilisation to-day not only surpasses her own civilisation of a thousand years ago, but also the culture of many European countries. All this has taken place thanks to science. From the time of the discovery of science men began to use instruments, i.e. first they accumulated knowledge, and then applied it in practice. This period I call the period of " understanding before the performance of action." This is the third period of evolution.

As science is the systematic knowledge of rules and facts, every piece of knowledge may be a deception unless it is consecrated by the scientific method. The Chinese people in years gone by thought that the sky " is round and moves, while the earth is square and stands motionless." See what an irony ! With the help of science we see that all this is false. In China there is the custom of calling an adopted son " the son of a caterpillar," as it is supposed that a wasp has not its own young, but, as a popular story has it, always has a caterpillar in its nest. In reality this is not so : the wasp first takes a caterpillar into its nest, then, by letting a certain poisonous fluid into the head of the caterpillar, makes it motionless but does not kill it. Then it lays its eggs in the body of the caterpillar. Thus the caterpillar cannot crawl away, for it has been deprived of the power of motion and it cannot decay, since it is alive ; it can only become a food for the wasp's young which hatch out of the eggs in the caterpillar's body. It is the same as the anæsthetic given by a surgeon to a patient, but it is a case of a wasp and a cater-pillar. We see that the wasp invented this anæsthetic many thousands of year before our doctors. The wasp required it to prevent the caterpillar from crawling away, and at the same time to prevent the decay of the body it needed for the welfare of its young. This circumstance may also help us to convince ourselves that " action is easy but knowledge is difficult," since the wasp is quite ignorant, but acts ; so that we see that the theory is justified in application, not only to men, but also to insects.

As mentioned above, the evolution of mankind falls into three periods : " action without understanding," " understanding after action," and " understanding before action." If we divide people according to their individualities, we shall find three groups : the first, those who create and invent (they are called pioneers and leaders), the second, those who transmit or disseminate new ideas and inventions (these are called disciples), and the third are those who carry out what they receive from the people of the first two groups, without doubting and without hesitating (these are called unconscious performers and people of action). All these three groups are mutually interdependent and closely connected with one another.

Since the Han and Chien dynasties, the Chinese cannot be compared with their forefathers, the men of the Great Wall and the Grand Canal. This is very regrettable.

After our Chinese Revolution the time of wholesale reconstruction has arrived. Now is the time to carry out in real life that which we know, which we can fulfil, and which we must fulfil. A country with a population of over 400 millions, with a territory of more than 429,000 square miles, with such extensive natural riches as few possess, undoubtedly has a great field for development. If the men of my day will sincerely combat harmful ideas, particularly those which have fettered the energy of the Chinese people for a thousand years, i.e. the formula " knowledge is easy but action is difficult," and at the same time bend their

KNOWLEDGE AND REVOLUTIONARY ACTION

energies to agitation for the fundamental watchwords of our Revolution (nationalism, democracy,
the foundations of the Chinese Constitution),
China will rapidly become a strong and mighty
Republic.

In proof of my assertions, and to oblige the
Chinese to renounce harmful ideas, I shall acquaint
my readers with the revolution of the United
States of America and with the reforms of Japan.

The revolution of the United States of America
was carried out by three million people, scattered
over thirteen provinces along the shores of the
Atlantic Ocean. They were placed at a dis-
advantage for a civil struggle, since they had to
fight savage Indian tribes on one side and a
powerful enemy, who blockaded them, on the
other. Nevertheless, the Americans fought the
British to the death for eight years, and finally
secured from Great Britain the recognition of
the independence of America, which thus was
transformed from a colony into a republic. If
we compare the conditions in which the Americans
had to begin their revolution with the conditions
of the Chinese Revolution, we shall realise that
their path was more difficult than ours. Science
at that time was not so developed as at the present
day, the population of America represented only
one-hundredth of ours, and naturally the Americans
had less possibilities for setting up a new State
than we have. But they fought against Great
Britain and won. This was a hundred odd years

ago. Now the United States is one of the mightiest Powers in the world.

Now about the transformation of Japan into a modern State. When Japan began her reforms, she was a very weak country, with a population not more than one-tenth the size of ours, and with a territory equivalent to one of our provinces. If we consider the degree of her civilisation at the time, we must admit that it was much more recent than that of China to-day. And yet now Japan is one of the strongest Powers in the world. Her people have given up their old prejudices, they have learned the lessons of the West, reformed their administration, created an army and fleet, organised their finances, and have done all this in the space of fifty years. In order to become a Great Power, Japan took only fifty years in place of the hundred which were required by the United States of America. Consequently, if we base ourselves on these standards and relationships China can become a very powerful State if she concentrates on the work of her transformation for the space of, say, ten years. I think that this space is sufficient. It is, undoubtedly. If the reader doubts this, I shall illustrate it by the case of the reforms in Siam.

Siam was originally one of the countries ruled by China. At the period of the reforms there were only eight million people in Siam, and she occupied a territory not larger than our province of Szechuan. Only three-fifths of the population were Chinese, while the remainder of the people were for the most part semi-savage tribes. Nearly the whole industrial and commercial activity of Siam was concentrated in the hands of Chinese. But Siam lay between British Burma and French Indo-China. This placed her in a difficult position. If, twenty years ago, Siam had not undertaken great reforms, she could never have existed as an independent State.

The King of Siam and his Court decided to follow the example of Japan. Reforms, adopted in time, saved the country from partition and preserved its independence. Only after twenty years of reforms did Siam become a civilised and independent country. Its international prestige to-day is much better than ours. In Asia there are only two independent countries—Japan and Siam. China is called only a semi-independent State. Why? Because the subjects of Western states still enjoy in China special treaty privileges. For example, they have the right to live in their own special parts of our cities, the so-called " concessions " and " treaty ports," and to be governed by the laws of their own country. And above all, our sovereign right to the maritime customs is still in the hands of foreigners, while Japan and Siam are free from these unprofitable obligations.

Siam became a strong country in a shorter time than Japan, Japan in a shorter time than the United States of America. We may anticipate that China will become a strong country in an even shorter space of time than Japan and Siam, as it is situated in more favourable conditions than they.

I return to my theory of " the easiness of action and the difficulty of knowledge." Let us suppose, reader, that you now accept this theory, it will still be natural for you to ask me, how can it be applied, i.e. how should we act and work ? The reply to this question will be very short. It will depend entirely on the faith of the disciples and followers in their forerunners the pioneers, and on the approval of their contemporaries.

I have already pointed out that three groups of people inspire and develop civilisation : the pioneers and forerunners—the inventors and thinkers, who make great discoveries ; the disciples and followers—the people who disseminate and agitate ; and the men of action—the performers, who carry out in practice what has been discovered and invented. The latter may be quite un-acquainted with knowledge. It is foolish to say : " There are no men of action : " no, there are many. Many of our Party comrades in the Kuomintang have the habit of saying : " So-and-so is a theoretician, and So-and-so is a man of action." This is wrong : everyone can be a theoretician, everyone can be a man of action. To say that only one or two men are practical, active workers in the revolutionary movement, is the greatest mistake. If we look at many fine buildings belonging to foreigners in Shanghai, we see at once that they were built by our workmen who knew absolutely nothing about plans and the art of building : the plans were drawn up by foreigners. The latter did the work of planning : they may be called the inventors and seekers. Similarly, in the building up of a country it is easy to find men of action, but very difficult to find people who can work out plans of reconstruction.

The modern Chinese, or shall we say their majority, treat the foundations of knowledge with contempt and value action highly. This is not quite justifiable. In our age of science we must know how to value knowledge as well as performance. Men of action do not at all require to be men steeped in knowledge, it is sufficient to be able to carry out what is required. If this idea of the modern Chinese lasts some time longer, it will corrupt many promising young people. Moreover, it is just as senseless as for a chemist to revere a maker of bean jelly, instead of giving attention to the discoverer of the principles underlying the preparation of this food ; or for a doctor to despise the inventor of anæsthetics, but to revere the wasp.

I regret very much to record the fact that the whole youth of China suffers from this defect of thought. Consequently, there is no public opinion leading civilisation along the path of progress, but an exactly opposite phenomenon is to be observed. By such ways we can scarcely find the true path

for the political and economic regeneration of
China. This is the real reason why the Chinese
Republic does not flourish and China does not
emerge from stagnation, notwithstanding that we
established a republican form of government after
our democratic revolution. Therefore I consider
myself bound to win the minds of my fellow-
countrymen and women away from the preconceived idea which has taken root in them that
" knowledge is easy but action is difficult," and
to the idea that " action is easy but knowledge
is difficult," by means of repeated explanations
and proofs. I hope that they will all abandon
their preconceived idea and dogmatic phrase,
which seems, in a certain measure, correct to people
with a superficial mind, but which in reality is
unquestionably false. If my work is successful,
the future of China will be bright, and our country
will in a short time take its place amongst the
mighty world Powers of to-day.

CHAPTER IV

PROBLEMS OF THE
REVOLUTIONARY REORGANISATION OF CHINA

AT the present time, in the epoch of the triumph of science, every creator must first comprehend his work and then begin carrying it out. His followers, to avoid mistakes and waste of time, and to achieve success in the work begun, must grasp the conclusions of their leader and, on the basis of these conclusions, draw up the principles and plans according to which work should proceed. Only in such conditions can our task be fulfilled successfully, despite all its complexity and vastness.

Thus, for example, at the present day there are being built aeroplanes of a very delicate and complicated pattern, wireless telegraph stations, or, say in America, a railway thousands of miles long. Again, the construction of the Suez and Panama canals were also gigantic undertakings. Nevertheless, when one is acquainted with scientific methods, when one has studied the plans drawn up by engineers and has become acquainted with all the accompanying conditions, the completion of these undertakings is not a very difficult task. All this has been established quite exactly by experience, and my fellow-countrymen must admit it. I believe that revolutionary creation must follow the path of modern progress, utilising the past experience of other countries, avoiding their mistakes and making use of their achievements : for only by maturely considering and appraising from all sides the experience of revolutions in other countries and amongst other peoples can we hope to build up revolutionary tactics.

I distinguish three phases of development of the revolution : the first, military government ; the second, preparatory ; the third, constitutional reconstruction.

The first phase covers the period of destruction. In this period it is proposed to introduce martial law. The revolutionary troops must finally destroy the autocracy of the Tai-Tsing dynasty, drive out the corrupt bureaucracy, root out evil practices, get rid of unjust slavery, wipe out the poison of opium, eradicate the superstition of magic and fortune-telling, and abolish likin (internal customs duties).

In the second phase, that of preparation, the task will be to establish local self-government and facilitate the consolidation of the power of the people, making the country the unit of local self-government, subdivided into villages and rural districts. Every county, after the enemy has been cleared from its territory and military operations have ceased, will have to publish a provisional constitution to determine the rights and duties of citizens, as well as the rights of the revolutionary government. Three years later the citizens will elect their county authority. If the county succeeds in rooting out evil as described above, and one-half of the citizens realise and understand the three principles of the democratic theory, and are loyal to the Republic, the county authorities will be able to ascertain the numbers of the population of the county, determine the house tax, organise the police, public hygiene, the means of communication—all according to the principles established by the Constitution. Electing its county authorities and thus becoming a true self-governing unit, the county may count on the revolutionary government taking up a favourable attitude toward it, and granting it all its constitutional rights under the provisional constitution. If, after the lapse of six years, peace has been established throughout the country, all the self-governing counties will have to elect one deputy each to constitute a great National Assembly. The task of this Assembly will be to establish five Chambers, in the spirit of the " Constitution of Five Forms," to organise the work of government : the first administrative, the second legislative, the third judicial, the fourth examinatory, the fifth for control and inspection.

After the adoption of the Constitution, the citizens in the counties will elect by ballot a

President to organise the Administrative Chamber, and will also elect deputies to constitute the Legislative Chamber : the other three Chambers will be appointed by the President, with the agreement of the Legislative Chamber. All the Chambers are responsible not to the President but to the National Assembly. The resignation of members of the Chambers can take place only upon their indictment by the Chamber of Inspection and Control before the National Assembly, while the dismissal of members of the Chamber of Inspection and Control is possible after their accusation by the National Assembly. The powers and duties of the National Assembly consist in exercising supervision of the transformation of the Constitution and eliminating unworthy public employees. The qualifications for membership of the National Assembly and of the Chambers will be established through the medium of the Chamber of Examinations.

After the confirmation of the Constitution, the election of the President, and the election of the Chambers, the revolutionary government shall hand over power to the President, and the preparatory phase may be considered at an end from this moment.

The third phase is the period of the completion of the Revolution. In this period it is proposed to achieve constitutional government. In this period the self-governing counties must begin to exercise their direct civic rights : the citizens enjoy adult suffrage in the management of their county, the right of deciding political questions, and also the right of dismissing Government officials. This is the constitutional phase, i.e. the period in which revolutionary reconstruction is completed. This in general outline is the scheme of revolutionary tactics which I recommend.

From the moment of the establishment of the Republic, I strove with all my forces for the application of these revolutionary tactics in order to attain the ultimate aims of the Chinese Revolution and the realisation of the three principles of democracy. But however much I explained and defended, my Party comrades found these tactics impracticable. My ideas were too lofty for the comprehension of my comrades, whose level of political intelligence was too low for that time, and I involuntarily suffered through this. Revolutionary construction and revolutionary destruction must be closely co-ordinated and go hand in hand. If revolutionary construction is not begun immediately after revolutionary destruction, all will perish. The task of revolutionary construction must be imposed on the President. Therefore I suggested that after the formation of the Nanking Government an armistice should be proposed and a Peace Conference convened.

At the present time, when, after all the events that occurred, circumstances have changed, there are many people who criticise me and consider that I ought not to have entered into peace negotiations in the first year of the Republic and voluntarily given up my post as President. However, even if I had continued to be President— but the majority of my Party comrades after the period of revolutionary destruction would not abide by their revolutionary oath and would not submit to the guidance of their leader, who could unite all the revolutionaries of China—it would still have been impossible to realise the aims of the Revolution. The result would have been only that new officials would replace the old, which could scarcely bring China anything new in the sense of a reform of the Government or the strengthening of her economic power. And since matters stood thus, there was scarcely any need for me to retain the post of President.

Some who do not understand the conditions of the Chinese Revolution consider that my power was less at that time than that of Yuan-Shih-Kai, and therefore I was forced to enter on the path of reconciliation; while some slanderers even asserted that I received a bribe of a million from Yuan-Shih-Kai, and therefore yielded him up the Presidency. At the present time I do not need to defend myself, as the slander is obvious without this. After all, if I had been mercenary, undoubtedly it is not for a million that I should have given up my post as President : do you not see how much a Tuchun lays by in a single year, or how much a divisional commander swallows up ? With regard to the suggestion that in the first year of the Republic my power was less than that of Yuan-Shih-Kai, this also is scarcely worth arguing, as the Republic at that time already controlled fifteen provinces, the Shantung and Honan Kuomintang were also in revolt, and the accession of Chihli was delayed for three months by military considerations. There can be for us no doubt that the whole country was determined as one man to get rid of the monarchy.

But even if we do not take this into account, and only take the facts of the past and appraise them, it will be clear that I adopted the method of conciliation by no means out of fear of the power of Yuan-Shih-Kai. Before the victory of the Revolution I suffered ten defeats, but my revolutionary spirit has never enfeebled as a result. In the second year of the Republic, Yuan-Shih-Kai united the whole country, and I went on working, without occupying myself with politics : but when he brutally murdered Sun-Chiao-Jen, could I remain passive ? Without having a single soldier at my disposal, I declared the necessity of fighting Yuan-Shih-Kai. Unfortunately, my comrades in the south did not support me seriously and did not send help in good time, and therefore I was defeated. After the defeat of my revolt, all my colleagues were overcome by despair, not daring to raise again the banner of revolution. But I, knowing that Yuan-Shih-Kai's aspirations were to become emperor, brought the Kuomintang to a state of complete preparedness, and despatched its members throughout all the provinces to agitate against the restoration of the autocracy.

The spirit of revolt was sown by me in the people so effectively that it was sufficient for the Restoration to show its face for it immediately to be rebuffed by the efforts of the whole people. From all this it can be seen that I renounced the Presidency, not for fear of the power of Yuan-Shih-Kai, but because I could not carry out the tasks of revolutionary reconstruction. Only in this way can my determination on, and striving for, the work of revolutionary reconstruction be understood.

What are the problems of revolutionary reconstruction? Revolutionary reconstruction is emergency construction, and this in its turn is hurried construction. Therefore it must seek permanence and follow the natural social tendencies, since construction that is guided purely by the requirements of the moment will not always coincide with the tasks of the Revolution. The Revolution has its own emergency work of destruction, as in the case of the overthrow of the monarchy and the destruction of the Imperial regime. But side by side with this emergency destruction there must also be emergency construction, as they accompany each other like a pair of legs or wings

in motion. From the moment of the foundation
of the Republic we had already left the stage of
emergency destruction, but had not a subsequent
period of emergency construction : and this was
the source of the misfortunes which were showered
upon us : the cruel rule of officials, the internecine
struggle of politicians, etc. The Chinese had no
means of eliminating all this. In a time of
emergency, emergency construction is also required,
and only then can the people be accustomed to
new tasks.

This is extremely important for revolutionary
tactics. In order to understand it, I will direct
your attention to the revolutions which preceded
the Chinese. The most gigantic were the American
and French Revolutions. America has not altered
the system of government she established after
the Revolution for over a hundred years, and,
with the exception of the struggle of South against
North, she had no great civil wars. Thus it may
be said that, after the Revolution, the govern-
mental structure which was established did not
change, and that during the many years' existence
of the Republic perpetual peace has existed,
culture has progressed, and an extraordinary
economic development has taken place.

But after the French Revolution, great troubles
took place, and the State structure of France
was changed five times. In France there was
twice a monarchy and three times a republic,
and the Republic was only firmly established

eighty years after the first Revolution. How is this to be explained ? Many say that Washington had a virtuous and conciliatory character, and therefore when founding their Republic the Americans succeeded in avoiding all perils. Napoleon I had the audacious idea of subjugating the whole world, and therefore his autocracy suffered defeat, and the idea of a republic triumphed. But revolutions are not made in the interests of individuals : they are the result of the revolutionary action of the masses. Washington and Napoleon were by no means the chief factors in the American and French Revolutions. When the Americans found the English yoke unbearable, they invited Washington to be their leader and rose in revolt. In France it was already after the Revolution that Bonaparte emerged from the army to take power into his own hands. Both these men were raised up by the wave of revolution.

America in the past was a huge prairie continent. The English colonised this territory only 200 years ago. They were always endowed with a spirit of fearlessness and contempt of dangers, and with a capacity for self-government. When they arrived in America, they immediately organised their machinery of self-government, which later became the thirteen States. These were ruled by England, but, as the proverb has it, " the whip will not strike at a long distance," and they were only nominally subordinated to Britain. They soon felt that the taxes imposed on them by the metropolis were burdensome. This forced all the thirteen States to unite for the purpose of resistance, in consequence of which the American Revolution took place. After a bloody eight years' war, the Americans secured their independence and set up a republic—the United States of America.

Even before they won independence, the thirteen American States had a highly developed local self-government, and therefore, in achieving independence, they completed their political structure, since its basis was strongly developed local autonomy. Other parts of America, Central and Southern, tried for a hundred years to follow the example of the United States, in throwing off the yoke of their mother-country and establishing republics. They were subjected to the intervention of foreign States, and were very often threatened with a restoration. Nevertheless there is not a single monarchy in the New World. America has washed off all the old dirt, and has freed herself from monarchism for ever.

This is not the case in France. France was one of the foremost European States, with a very courageous and cultured people. Moreover, before the Revolution the French people passed through a hundred years' propaganda of the rights of the people and philosophical teachings. Although she followed the lessons taught by America,

France still proved unable to arrive at a democratic republic immediately after the Revolution. Why ? Wherein lie the reasons for this ? The fact is that the form of government in the West had long been monarchical, and State policy had for long been one of centralisation. France had not the virgin soil of the New World with its basis of local self-government.

The defects of our own China are similar to those of France, but in addition the political intelligence of our citizens is immeasurably lower than that of the French at the time of the French Revolution, just as is their capacity for self-government. Hence arises the question, how then do I strive in China to arrive directly through the Revolution at a republican constitution ? But it is for this very purpose that I propose a pre-paratory period—just in order to get out of this difficult situation. During this preparatory period I propose a provisional constitutional government, and also the introduction of local self-government.

Unfortunately, my comrades at that time did not understand these reasons, and did not work to carry out my plans, and only used the name of my provisional constitution to confirm the Provisional Constitution of the Republic, consider-ing that the goal might be approached by other paths. All of them, undoubtedly, were badly mistaken at the time when they opposed my tactical plan as one which was difficult to carry

out—without preliminarily thinking the question
out thoroughly.

At the time when I was preaching the Revolution
and the idea of setting up a Chinese Republic, the
European and American scholars for the most
part considered this quite unrealisable for China,
supporting their views by references to past
history. In the first year of the Chinese Republic,
when travelling through London, I met a famous
Englishman who had travelled through China
high and low, was well acquainted with the
situation and customs of our country, and had
written a great deal about her. His book *Changing
China*, is very good. This Englishman heard that
I preach the transformation of China into a
republic and, conceiving great doubts on this
score, visited me at my hotel for the special
purpose of talking with me on this subject. We
argued for several days without being able to
come to an agreement. But when I outlined to
him my theory about the three periods of
revolutionary tactics, he immediately agreed with
me, saying: " Yes, with such a plan you can
escape the tyranny of autocracy, militarism and
politicians, and their infringement of the rights of
the people. I consider it my duty, now and for the
future, to support you in my articles." In actual
fact, so soon as the Revolution broke out in
Wuchang, the whole Western Press wrote that my
plan for the establishment of a republic must be
realised in the near future, and every friend of

China must await this moment with impatience. All this, of course, was an echo of the campaign carried out by the above-mentioned Englishman in the London Press.

It is often said that China with its ignorant population will not be able to establish a republican administration. A well-known American scholar, Goodenough, using this argument, tried to incite Yuan-Shih-Kai to restore the monarchy. At one time the Chinese marvelled greatly at this, failing to understand how a republican professor could advocate a monarchy, but I knew that the Americans, having had the experience of a republic, had learned from experience what unintelligent and uneducated citizens mean. Every emigrant after living some time in America enjoys the rights of citizenship. After the emancipation of the negroes, the latter were also given rights of citizenship in America. But the American politicians took advantage of this and committed abominable misdeeds for a number of years, until a law was passed that illiterates were deprived of many civic rights. This is why American professors, hearing of the proposed foundation of a republic by the ignorant and politically backward Chinese people, bitterly shook their heads and said it was impossible.

According to the Goodenough psychology, they could not of course fail to observe the low level of political intelligence of the Chinese, soaked, moreover, in the poison of an age-old monarchy, and maintained in a lower stage of development than the former black slaves of America. The followers of Yuan-Shih-Kai also shouted about the impossibility of establishing a republic in China.

An ox can be taught to plough, a horse can be broken in to the saddle, but what can be said of man? Can we tell a father who is sending his child to school that the child does not know the Chinese characters and therefore must not go to school and learn? Is this logical? Just because he does not know the characters, he must immediately set about learning them. Moreover, modern humanity has already reached the youthful years of its progress, and therefore within it the ideas of freedom and equality are very developed. World ideas could not help reaching China, and therefore China to-day needs the Republic just as a child needs school. But China also needs good teachers and well-disposed friends for her studies. The Chinese people, which has just acquired a republican form of government, must have a far-seeing revolutionary government for its training. This applies particularly to the period of preparation and training, which will be a kind of transitional stage between monarchy and republic, such as China cannot avoid.

At the foundation of our "Revolutionary League," one of its members, being convinced of the difficulty of carrying out my revolutionary plan, said : " The Tai-Tsing dynasty gave a false constitution and a preparatory period of nine years, and now the plans of our Party also speak of nine years. But we consecrated our lives to the revolution in the hope that the power of the people will be established immediately ; if we shall have to wait another three years after the victory of the people, this will be too long." I replied that without this there is no hope of establishing a true republic. To-day eight years have gone by since the establishment of the Chinese Republic, but not only has the period of constitutional government not begun, but unfortunately it cannot yet be said that the Tai-Tsing dynasty has been torn up by the roots.

Some think that the six years of preparatory training which we propose bear a strong resemblance to the enlightened despotism preached by some so-called learned men. In reply to this I will say that the enlightened despotism has as its end an absolute monarchy, whereas our period of preparation and training has as its end the creation of a republic. This constitutes a colossal difference between them. During the Great War, for example, all the States which entered the war—both monarchies and republics—all as one man arrested the functioning of the constitution and introduced a military regime, under which all citizens were deprived of their liberties. The distribution of foodstuffs was handed over to the State, and, in those countries where there was insufficient food, the inhabitants sacrificed their lives for their fatherland and for victory. These peoples had already possessed a constitutional government, yet their constitution was limited. We who as yet have no Constitution, and are striving for constitutional guarantees by means of a revolutionary struggle, can only marvel that the European peoples agreed to such a limitation.

Eight years have now passed since the establishment of the Chinese Republic, and the members of our Party must in the course of these eight years have acquired a vast store of experience and knowledge. To-day they can recall my platform on the question of preparing and training the masses, and grasp its significance without labelling my ideas Utopian and impracticable. China has been for thousands of years under the retrograde yoke of a monarchy, and her people has grown up in oppression and deprived of sovereignty. At the very dawn of the Revolution, it determined to create its own constitutional republican State. Therefore it must go through a course of preparatory training, otherwise it cannot achieve its object.

America, when going to the aid of Philippine independence, also went along the path of establishing a period of training for the Philippines, with the development and strengthening of local self-government as its basis. Twenty years have gone by, and the Filipinos, once a semi-savage people, have become a cultured people. Local self-government in the Philippines is now extremely developed, the majority of the local government officials, with the exception of the Governor, are natives, and in the near future (probably) the Filipinos will secure complete independence. In the future, we can hope, they will not be distinguishable in culture from the most advanced European states. All this is the result of a policy of preparatory training.

Why did not America give the Filipinos independence at once, and forced them instead to go through a period of preparatory training? Because America had already had experience of disorders after a similar emancipation of the negroes, and her policy was based on her experience.

Our Chinese people have long been under the domination of a monarchy. The slave psychology has left in its soul a deep impression, which cannot be destroyed without first passing through a period of preparatory training. In order to wash off this old dirt of the past, and to partake of the modern conceptions of liberty and equality, the Chinese must work a great deal at their own improvement.

The Chinese Republic is a people's State: its Emperor is a people of 400 millions. The State officials, beginning with the President and ending with an ordinary sentry, are all public servants. The Chinese people of 400 millions was from ancient times a slave of the autocracy, and did not know in the past that it was master. When at last it did learn, for a long time it did not dare to be master. Yet sooner or later it must do so. What was it that gave the Chinese people the chance? Was it not the Revolution, which destroyed the Monarchy? In consequence of the fact that China for ages had not altered her form of government, the people turned out to be a new-born babe when it approached the task of reconstruction for the first time. The Kuomintang bore this infant, and is obliged to nurse it like a mother and train it, and only by training the people can it carry out its parental duty. And for this the period of preparatory training is necessary, so that the child can be given experience and trained up to years of discretion, up to the moment when it can take over power itself.

In ancient times a certain Chow-Guns, prepared and politically trained his youthful Emperor until he ascended the throne. Our Party must realise that under the monarchy the official servant trained his master for the acceptance of power, and it is natural that we must do the same with our master, the people, until it reaches years of discretion. Unfortunately, our Party at that time did not realise the necessity of this clearly enough; it renounced responsibility for the training of the people and did not carry out its revolutionary duty. The Chinese achieved in their revolutionary effort only the work of destruction, and were not able to carry through the work of construction. That is why, as a result of our struggle, we have to-day the name " Chinese Republic," and nothing more.

Wherein lie the reasons for the fact that the destructive part of the Chinese Revolution was crowned with success while its constructive part suffered defeat ? The root of the matter is in two things, namely, intelligence and ignorance. The Chinese long failed to realise that they were oppressed by the Manchu dynasty, and were in a condition of trance or intoxication, looking on revolution as some sort of disgusting injustice. But later, when the waves of revolution rolled over China the people became much more politically intelligent, and understood the necessity for overthrowing the Manchu dynasty and returning to power themselves. And if the old Manchu dynasty were now to return to power, it would meet with the resistance of the whole people. But very, very many amongst us know nothing of a conscious revolution, and even amongst members of the Kuomintang there are few persons who understand all its implications. Consequently, it is not surprising that we did not meet with as many difficulties in the revolt itself as we met with at the moment when we reached the problems of reconstruction.

The difficult has now been achieved, but the easy, on the other hand, has suffered defeat. What are the reasons for this ? The very fact that it was easy, and that the majority of the people did not know that it must be immediately applied in real life. That is why my plan of revolutionary reconstruction suffered defeat. Why do I call it easy ? Because after destruction had been completed, the forces of resistance were destroyed, and once these forces were destroyed, nothing was impossible for us : in everything we had perfect liberty in comparison with the epoch before the period of destruction. But the Chinese, unfortunately, did not think of the next period. I knew that the revolution against the Tai-Tsing dynasty was necessary in the name of the salvation of the country, and therefore embraced it, not reckoning with dangers and without observing its difficulties. Hence, when the period of destruction closed, revolutionary reconstruction seemed an easy thing to me. But the majority of my colleagues had not mastered revolutionary methods, and thought otherwise : and therefore the attempts at revolutionary construction failed.

When our " Revolutionary League " was being set up to organise the Chinese Revolution, we first of all advocated its ideas by propaganda, and then, collecting together all who had determined to serve the Chinese people, swore to give effect to the idea of democracy based on " the three principles " (San-Min-Chu), in order to achieve our common aim—the establishment of a Chinese Republic. People who reject this public oath I do not recognise as revolutionaries. Some look on this revolutionary oath as a mere formality. However, the influence and power of the Kuomintang have grown extraordinarily. And its organisation has grown stronger because by our oath we have created a single heart of the Party. If this is how matters stand with the Party, the same can apply to the State.

It is very often said that the Chinese people resemble scattered grains of sand. If we desire to collect these 400 millions of scattered individual grains, and create out of them a united State, strong in its unity, we cannot reject the idea of an oath. In all advanced and cultured countries, when changing one nationality for another, it is necessary to express by means of an oath one's loyalty to and respect for the State into which one is entering, and to express recognition of its constitution and readiness to bear all the obligations arising therefrom. Only after this can one be recognised as a citizen. Without this, you can live all your life in the country, and you will be regarded as a foreigner who cannot enjoy civic rights.

I consider that officials and members of the Chambers can enter into office only after taking the oath. When the form of government is changed, the new Government will undoubtedly require an oath of loyalty from all citizens, and will regard those who refuse as enemies who must be driven from the confines of the State. I take examples from the advanced countries of Europe. If we look at the European States constituted after the war, we can say that those of them have proved able to live which have been able to carry their State oaths of allegiance into effect, on the basis of the recognition of the Government by the majority of the people. In States which have not been able to apply an oath of allegiance, disorders and troubles do not cease. In China the same thing is going on to-day. It was just because of this that, when organising our Party, I put the oath and Party discipline in the forefront. When the Kuomintang set up the Republic, I, as its first President, first took the oath of allegiance, and ordered all civil and military officers immediately to take the oath as an expression of their devotion to the Republic. Unfortunately, our Party did not regard this as a matter of great urgency and importance, and protested against the immediate application of the oath of allegiance. This was a great mistake.

When, later on, Yuan-Shih-Kai succeeded me as President, he also did not pay particular attention to this question, and allowed my old oath to remain, with its words: " Down with the monarchy for ever, long live the Republic ! " When subsequently he betrayed the Revolution

and proclaimed himself emperor, these words of
the oath were turned against him. Not only we,
the Chinese revolutionaries, but the foreign Powers
also presented a Note of protest against the
restoration of the monarchy : and this was one
of the principal reasons why the monarchy of
Yuan-Shih-Kai collapsed. The monarchy of Yuan-
Shih-Kai could not but totter after the Note of
the Powers, who were obliged to send it after the
Kuomintang came out with a very reasoned
protest against his action. And our chief arguments amounted to this, that Yuan-Shih-Kai had
broken his oath.

Yuan-Shih-Kai was in the past a servant of the
monarchy, and did not hold republican ideas.
How then was it that the Kuomintang yielded
up to him the post of President, and itself sacrificed
the Republic, voluntarily surrendering it at first
and only later on beginning to fight for it ? All
this, undoubtedly, would have been very irre-
sponsible, were it not for the oath, on account
of which the Powers, in defence of justice,
intervened on behalf of the Republic and supported it. I ask : Is not the oath of allegiance
important ?

However, my Party comrades considered the
oath I proposed to be a matter of secondary
importance, and called me a visionary. From the
time of the formation of the Party I have always
stood for the oath. The cessation of the ceremony
of the oath, that foundation of law, was one of

the chief reasons for the failure of our revolutionary construction. If my Party comrades had not despised my words, in the subsequent development of the Republic we should have had the same as in the organisation of our Party, namely, that every official would have been bound to take an oath of allegiance to the Republic, and swear that he would support the Republic, defend the rights of the people, and strengthen the economic power of the country. Only after taking such an oath would he have been able to enjoy all civic rights, while otherwise he would have been regarded as a servant of the Tai-Tsing dynasty.

After the taking of the oath, every offence against the Republic must be punished according to law. At present the only State criminals are Yuan-Shih-Kai and a few members of the Kuomintang who took the oath and broke it : but all the other 400 million citizens bear no moral or legal responsibility before the Chinese Republic. The State is a vessel which collects into itself men's hearts, while State policy is the reflection of psychological factors. In order to have the possibility of transforming the emperor's subjects into citizens of the Republic, it is necessary first of all to demand from them an oath of allegiance. The Kuomintang, when creating the republican State, was not able to carry it through to a successful conclusion. This was why the Party at first possessed a colossal reserve of spiritual forces and energies, and achieved success in the

work of destruction, while after the establishment
of the Republic it lost all these qualities and
could not complete the tasks of revolutionary
reconstruction. This was the result of error.
They failed to create and to construct not because
they could not do so, but because they did not
know how to do so.

Therefore I say: " If you understand, undoubtedly you will be able to carry into effect."
Many consider my ideals too lofty, and my plan
for the establishment of the Republic too idealistic,
but they, themselves had no plans and did not
know how to act. That is why China now finds
herself in a condition of anarchy and destruction.
Precisely because of this the Chinese people was
plunged into an eight years' period of severe
suffering, which, far from bringing it closer to
the completion of revolutionary construction, has
only deepened its misery.

The responsibility for the failure of the Chinese
Revolution must fall not only on the Chinese revolutionaries, but also on all intelligent Chinese
citizens who would not shed their blood in the
front ranks of the Revolution. They were the
rearguard of the Revolution, whose task it was
to support the fighting revolutionaries. People of
China! Rise with one heart, with love for your
native land, to drive out the old and create the
new, repeat sincerely and truthfully the oath
of allegiance to the Chinese Republic which I have
taken:

" I, Sun-Yat-Sen, truthfully and sincerely take this public oath that from this moment I will destroy the old and build the new, and fight for the self-determination of the people, and will apply all my strength to the support of the Chinese Republic, the realisation of democracy through ' the three principles,' and to carry into effect ' the Fivefold Constitution,' for the progress of good government, the happiness and perpetual peace of the people, and for the strengthening of the foundations of the State, in the name of peace throughout the world."

SUN-YAT-SEN.

January 12,
8th Year of the Chinese Republic.

I have taken my oath. This oath should strictly be introduced by the Government, but at present, while the Republican Government has not yet introduced it, this ceremony cannot be performed. But I trust that all intelligent citizens in the organised self-governing counties will by joint endeavour take the oath immediately after setting up their governing bodies, and reinforce the text of the oath with their signature, reading the oath publicly to the people with their right hand raised in the air. After the citizens of one county have taken the oath, they should help those of the next county with the same purpose. Only after the oath is taken should a man be considered a citizen of the Chinese Republic, both legally and morally, and otherwise he should be considered an adherent of the Monarchy.

K   145

Will it be possible to establish a Republic, or not ? The answer depends entirely on whether our fellow-countrymen willingly or unwillingly perform the ceremony of an oath of allegiance to the Chinese Republic.

Chinese patriots, follow my example !

CHAPTER V

WHO WAS RIGHT?

(Letter from Chen-Yin-Shin to Huan-Kai-Tsiang)

BROTHER HUAN-KAI-TSIANG!

WITH my modest talents I have taken part in public affairs for years past, and have always met with the friendliest attitude from you. Last summer I was in hospital when you left for Japan and, despite my eager desire, could not see you and shake hands with you, as some little consolation for myself. Now we have been deprived of the opportunity of talking and expressing our ideas to one another personally. How unfortunately it has all turned out!

The other day I saw my Japanese friend Miasaki, who told me that you have once more plunged into political affairs, and I once again began to think of you a great deal.

Even before 1911, comrades Sun-Chiao-Jen and Tan-I-Kai, during their stay in Shanghai, declared that in our Party they regarded you as one of the most outstanding practical revolutionaries, while Sun-Yat-Sen they regarded as our best theoretician and idealogue. This undoubtedly expressed the opinion of the whole country. But there also exists the opinion that Sun-Yat-Sen is a great idealist, and this prejudice greatly hindered the application of his ideas; this is used as a reproach against Sun-Yat-Sen, this is made use of by his enemies to attack him. But all the facts of the past indicate that the biggest defeats suffered by our Party arose from the fact that we failed to appreciate Sun-Yat-Sen's ideas, considered them unattainable, and rose up against them. Thereby we brought about our own defeat.

To-day we must not show the same intolerance to Sun-Yat-Sen's ideas, in order not to repeat the errors of the past. Personally I want to wipe out my old mistakes and set forth all the history of our attacks on Sun-Yat-Sen, which led to our defeat. Will you not agree to hear it ?

At the time that Sun-Yat-Sen assumed the office of President the general position in our country was very confused and disordered, and he did not carry out his political plans, all the more because the economic condition of China was terrible. The Russian loan met with strong opposition from the Provisional Senate, while the population, considering it disastrous for their interests, regarded it as they would the plague or cholera. But in reality this loan by no means diverged from our interests, as we received 97 per cent. of the amount of the loan at 5 per cent. interest, while if we take the next loan concluded by Yuan-Shih-Kai with the Banking Consortium, there

we actually received only 82 per cent. at 5 per
cent. interest, and moreover the loan was guaran-
teed by the salt monopoly and lands in four
provinces, as well as the right of control over our
finances. I ask, which of these loans was advantageous and which disastrous, which was profitable
and which unprofitable ?

But Chinese public opinion did not discriminate,
and consequently ruined the economic policy of
the Government. Sun-Yat-Sen was placed in the
position of a man with hands tied, unable to carry
out his plans, while the State was in a very
dangerous condition. All this because we stub-
bornly maintained a wrong point of view and
distrusted the fundamental principles of Sun-
Yat-Sen. This is first. Then, after the Nanking
Peace Conference, when Yuan-Shih-Kai was to
be elected President, Sun-Yat-Sen at that time put
forward three chief points. First, that Yuan-
Shih-Kai should assume the Presidency in Nanking,
as he feared and foresaw many misunderstandings
between the as yet not finally reconciled North
and South. In the interests of maintaining the
unity of the country, he considered it essential that
Yuan-Shih-Kai should take office precisely at
Nanking, to unite North and South, to strengthen
confidence in Yuan-Shih-Kai amidst our Party
(the Kuomintang), and also to evoke loyalty on
his part.

Secondly, the Republic ought to transfer its
capital to Nanking because Pekin is a city plunged

in monarchical lethargy, which the sound of revolutionary bells cannot dissipate, a city of corrupt and criminal bureaucracy, which cannot be washed away by the waters of rivers. This city must lose its privileges. Only when the capital is changed will it be possible to tear out all the criminal roots of the monarchy.

Thirdly, the organisation of a republican government cannot be entrusted to Yuan-Shih-Kai, relying only on the act of abdication of the Tai-Tsing dynasty, as, according to the Provisional Constitution, the abdication could take place only after a decision of the people's representatives, and not by agreement between the former Tai-Tsing dynasty and Yuan-Shih-Kai.

These three arguments advanced by Sun-Yat-Sen were extremely well-founded, and he spared neither strength nor health in defending them. And if, later on, Yuan-Shih-Kai renounced his former words about his intention to assume the Presidency at Nanking and to give full self-government to the people, and made an attempt to overthrow the Republic, this was not the fault of Sun-Yat-Sen, because China came to this after renouncing his fundamental political plans.

We have to admit that we rejected them for extremely varied reasons ; but I consider the most important of all to have been the insufficient political intelligence of the members of our Party. In consequence of this we did not support Sun-

Yat-Sen's programme and political plans. This was our second offence against Sun-Yat-Sen.

After he left the post of President, he was in favour of our Party entirely leaving the field of politics, and occupying itself particularly with the education of the people, the improvement of our industry, the consolidation of a firm and permanent foundation for the Republic, yielding the fullness of political power to Yuan-Shih-Kai. At that time, thinking this to be empty chatter, we opposed this plan and, furthermore, interfered in the administrative and other affairs of the Government. Thereby we came into violent opposition to the Government, which aroused the fury of Yuan-Shih-Kai and the suspicion of our country. We were not able to carry into effect the ideas with which Sun-Yat-Sen, the loyal servant of the people, was imbued, and in this lies our third offence against him.

About all this one can say that it was due to the insufficient enlightenment of the members of our Party, and was far from being the mistake of you and me alone. When the enquiry into the murder of Sun-Chiao-Jen began, Sun-Yat-Sen had just returned to Shanghai. Learning that Yuan-Shih-Kai was restoring the monarchy and breaking faith with the Republic, he swore to remove him. His plan was the following : first of all, an alliance with Japan. This alliance was to weaken the forces of Yuan-Shih-Kai and strengthen the forces of our Party, as Japan is an Eastern Power and a neighbour, and friendly relations with her would be a blessing for our country. " If Japan helps me, victory will be on my side : if she helps Yuan-Shih-Kai, he will conquer "—these were the very words of Sun-Yat-Sen. Considering an alliance with Japan to be a question of particular importance, Sun-Yat-Sen decided to go to Japan in person. But I and a few more comrades were very hostile to this plan, and tried by every means to prevent his departure, while some reproached Sun-Yat-Sen with being too careless of his prestige. Meanwhile Yuan-Shih-Kai through his supporters, sent to Tokyo, Sun-Bao-Tsi and Li-Shen-To, had already achieved what Sun-Yat-Sen feared, and our plan of an alliance with Japan was defeated.

Sun-Yat-Sen thought that the Kuomintang must strive for an alliance with Japan, as the latter alone of all the Asiatic States had been able to transform herself into a great and powerful country, and in order to come closer to her and learn from her.

Again, he had the idea of an immediate war. In view of the fact that Yuan-Shih-Kai had acquired a great deal of power, he was moving armies from place to place quite freely. Sun-Yat-Sen proposed that we should strike a blow with lightning rapidity and take him by surprise, as in the even of delay the right moment will be lost. These were the words of Sun-Yat-Sen. But we procrastinated and, not having faith in him, insisted on this question being settled in a constitutional way, opposing a declaration of war. This was our fourth wrong to Sun-Yat-Sen.

The case of the murder of Sun-Chiao-Jen was dragged out, since Yuan-Shih-Kai did not wish to reckon with the law. The Five Power loan was ratified without the sanction of Parliament, Throughout the country there were furious protests. And we hoped that, under the pressure of these protests, Yuan-Shih-Kai would have to yield to the wishes of the people and renounce the loan.

Sun-Yat-Sen considered that Parliament was a mere talking-shop, that the law was powerless, that the provincial authorities, for the most part subservient to Yuan-Shih-Kai, would not long maintain themselves in their previous positions, and that to solve the problem it was essential to resort to force of arms, as only such arguments would be understood by a traitor who had surrounded himself with troops. The measures prepared by Sun-Yat-Sen consisted firstly in immediately drawing the attention of the Public Prosecutor to the cases which had been hushed up, and secondly in declaring to the Banking Consortium that the whole people did not recognise the loan. When the Consortium received this declaration from Sun-Yat-Sen, it ceased payments in respect of the loan. Further, Sun-Yat-Sen by telegraph ordered the province of Kwantung to declare its independence. But the province did not obey. He ordered me to declare the independence of Shanghai, but I objected, considering that the place was too insignificant in respect of its area, and inconvenient for offering resistance.

At this moment the fleet arrived and declared its independence. Sun-Yat-Sen was the first to welcome this. Later on, when it became known that the Northern troops were approaching Shanghai, I put forward the plan of a sudden attack by sea, which was supported by Sun-Yat-Sen : but you thought this plan unwise. Later still, when the fleet, by orders of Yuan-Shih-Kai, set out for Yangtai, in the province of Shantung, Sun-Yat-Sen wanted to prevent this, saying : " If the fleet helps me, I shall be victorious : if it helps Yuan-Shih-Kai, he will. I want to use its support, and will try by all means in my power to keep it here, since if it goes to Yangtai it will undoubtedly go over to the side of Yuan-Shih-Kai." You and I imagined that, as the fleet had declared its loyalty to us in the past, it would remain loyal in the future. The fleet left for Yangtai : there it fell into a trap, being bombarded by land batteries : and it went over to the side of Yuan-Shih-Kai.

Being in favour of a declaration of the independence of the Kwantung province Sun-Yat-Sen, decided immediately to leave for the south to take charge of all operations, appointing us, a few comrades who were acquainted with military affairs, to be at your disposal. But the necessary moment had gone by. All Sun-Yat-Sen's plans for bringing the loan to nought and overthrowing Yuan-Shih-Kai were unsuccessful, owing to the delay which had taken place. Public opinion was suppressed, hopes of victory were defeated by the power of money, the Powers' confidence in us was undermined, the law did not move against Yuan-Shih-Kai, and the loan of two milliards to cover the State deficit was used by Yuan-Shih-Kai to buy arms, equipment and food, to corrupt members of Parliament, and to reward traitors for the suppression of the South and the execution of members of our Party. If, at the time he had abolished the post of President, we had adopted the plan of Sun-Yat-Sen and had declared the independence of a number of provinces, it was still uncertain on whose side would have been the victory, as at that time the army of the allied provinces numbered 100,000, Li-Tun (the Northern commander) had not yet reached Kiangsi, and nothing had yet been heard of Tuan-Dsi-Jui in the south. We ought to have attacked the traitors with fresh and vigorous forces and wiped them off the face of the earth. Unfortunately, the province of Kwantung did not declare its independence at the time when the loan was being floated, and when it was not a matter of great difficulty to abolish the Tuchunate (the office of provincial governor instituted after the rstfi Revolution). Once the loan had been granted, however, the Powers began to assist Yuan-Shih-Kai, and after this the Northern troops began their steady advance against the South. Thus the idea of " the conquest of the North " proved belated. This was our fifth offence against Sun-Yat-Sen.

Sun-Yat-Sen's mind always went far ahead, piercing the future. I always blindly went against him, while you, although you accepted his ideas, always expressed doubt about their practicability. With my meagre intelligence, I always was imbued with the prejudice that Sun-Yat-Sen was an idealist, and therefore, whatever he proposed, always seemed to me far removed from reality, and consequently I always joined with you and your opposition. But who could know that the Chinese proverbs : " Once having lost an inch, you will lose an ell later on," or : " Don't forget the affairs of the past, they will serve as a teacher for you in the future " could be applied to affairs of State ? Unfortunately, I do not know your opinion on this matter.

So far as I am concerned, I can say that I should like to work with you and therefore would like to exchange a few thoughts with you. In my opinion, human intelligence is perfected in the course of time, and if old mistakes are recognised, they may be avoided for the future, and also if you can learn anything valuable from another, there is no shame in obeying him. Further I believe that the idea is the mother of reality, as, for example, when Sun-Yat-Sen twenty years ago propagated the idea of revolution and at that time nearly all the citizens of our country were against him, but after twenty years his ideas received recognition. If we had recognised his ideas twenty years ago, there would not have been that much delay in translating them into real life, and if we had acted in full co-operation, probably we could have achieved success. I consider Sun-Yat-Sen's ideas to be practicable in the measure of the attitude we take up towards them.

Sun-Yat-Sen used to say that " looking into the past, we can understand the future," while we " were always looking in the Western corner of the earth for what we had lost in the Eastern " (i.e. too late).

You, of course, greatly surpass me in intelligence, so that my words may seem childish prattle to you, and therefore I must make a great effort in order to express myself fully.

Sun-Yat-Sen said that the work of the Revolution may be accomplished within the space of the next five years. In fact, in the present condition of our country, when the sufferings of the people have reached their limit, when disorders do not cease and the troops rage, when the corruption and dissoluteness of those in authority truly bring the country to a state of chaos, it can still be said that the wheel will come full circle, and that it will be urgently necessary to take advantage of the right moment to revolt, and by a lightning

stroke destroy the evil and restore justice. Therefore I say that nearly all the ideas of Sun-Yat-Sen
must be given effect, without waiting another
twenty years, while circumstances dictate their
application, just as was the case at the time of
the overthrow of the Manchu dynasty. The
organisation of Chinese revolutionaries into a
single Party is the urgent problem of the present
time.

Our enemies did not know that the secret
society we set up after 1900 became the Kuomintang, and that, although externally the Party
widened the sphere of its influence and greatly
strengthened its forces, in reality it still had no
definite characteristics and was extraordinarily
varied in its composition. This was very vital,
as even the Chinese proverb has it : " If you
put the aromatic plant ' siun ' and the stinking
weed ' yu ' into one pot, you will smell no sweet
aroma."

Some of our comrades understood Sun-Yat-Sen's
aims and plans of organisation very well. He was
right in his indication of the way to change the
machinery of our Party, and in putting forward
the question of the oath and Party discipline.
He was right in considering that the infringement
of the oath and discipline led to the defeat of the
Revolution, as some members of the Party
unconsciously distorted the idea of true liberty,
and therefore the people did not enjoy the blessings
of equality after the Revolution. These persons

by their disorderly conduct and struggle for privileges forgot their duty to the Revolution and did not submit to established regulations. And when no one submits to anyone else, it is extremely difficult to attain unity of aim in the Party. Therefore Sun-Yat-Sen was profoundly right in supposing that we must submit to a single leadership, in order to achieve unity of action and the proper distribution of functions. This was needed, not in order to oppress anyone, but in order to put an end to the self-willed acts of many comrades.

I consider that everyone who desires to achieve the objects of the Revolution must respect the views of Sun-Yat-Sen as " the constellations respect the North Star." Just like a ship, we must have our pilot to determine our course. Otherwise if there are comrades who oppose Sun-Yat-Sen in the future in the same way as he was opposed in the past, in the future also all the plans of Sun-Yat-Sen will suffer the same defeat. Therefore my opinion is that to keep our oath to the revolution and to obey the instructions of Sun-Yat-Sen is our direct obligation.

In conclusion, I will say that many of our differences are due to the great distance which has divided us, and to the distortion of our ideas by other persons in transmission. But as our aims are united, I should like to grasp your hand and join with you to fight our common enemy—the terrible python who has seized the throat of our long-suffering country in his deadly coils.

But enough. I feel that my words cannot express all my thoughts, and I throw aside my pen.

CHEN-YIN-SHIN.

Spring,
4th Year of the Chinese Republic (1915).

CHAPTER VI

THE CAUSES OF CHINA'S POVERTY

SOMEONE said to me : " If matters are as you say, then at the present time, since modern culture is founded on science, we must first of all study a subject thoroughly before we can begin to carry out any of our plans. It is impossible to transform China into a modern State until the whole Chinese people has received education. This follows from your own words, when you say that action or realisation is not difficult in itself, but it is knowledge that is difficult, or, in the words of the ancient sages, ' tens and maybe hundreds of years are required for the diffusion of universal education.' Yet you imagine that China can immediately, by a single jump, reach the position of a powerful and wealthy nation, one amongst the world Powers. Where is the logic in your assertions ? "

To this I reply : the pupil first learns, and then knows how to act : yet, without having learned, he can also act. After all, in the days before science flourished nearly everything was first done, and then learned later ; and it was because, in those days, they did not understand everything completely, they imagined that things were concerned with " heavenly numbers " and " fate," and their achievements were not ascribed to human agency. But when mankind gradually grew up to intelligence and began to understand a great deal, it gradually began to free itself from superstition. And now that knowledge has expanded, it has become clear that the work of human hands surpasses all the so-called supernatural forces and predetermined things, while the " heavenly numbers " are only the creation of human psychology. But although science has proved all this to us, nevertheless, in all things that people do, first action prevails and then comes understanding. Human development proceeds more on the lines of unconscious activity—this is a law of nature.

No development of science has so far been able to make any changes in this law. That is why, in the development of mankind, unconscious activity represents a very important factor : practice, experiment, investigation and risk are its principal motive forces. A pupil makes exercises and practices, he acts in order to attain knowledge. A scientist also makes experiments and conducts researches in order to clear up and learn the truth. The researcher or explorer makes his researches in a sphere unknown to him, and makes his discoveries there. A brave man who risks his life is also plunging into the unknown to attain his objects. From this it can be seen that in the carrying out of the unknown lies the stimulus to the development of culture and progress.

In application to nation-building, it must be said that if you are striving for the reorganisation of the State, and moreover by the path of revolution, then to act before your actions are fully understood is a matter, not only of possibility, but also of necessity. The majority of countries whose power has flourished, as for example the Great Powers, first acquired their strength, and only then began organising the education of their people. Speaking of China, we can say that our intelligence is quite sufficient to enable us to take our place, at one bound, in the ranks of the Great Powers. The obstacle to this lies, not in the fact that without learning you cannot act, but in the worthlessness of our Government and our officials. They commit many crimes, the worst of which is that they seek to advance only their personal avaricious interests and do not reckon in the least with the interests of the State or the nation. The tuchuns accumulate millions in a very short time by means of robbery, and none of them takes any heed that he is undermining the vital forces of his country. In the modern European countries, policy leads usually to the well-being and protection of the interests of the people. The citizens of the European states apply their energies to the organisation of agriculture and industry, the development of trade, and generally to strengthening the power of their country. With us in China things are the very opposite.

If our Government officials did not seek power for selfish ends, and did not commit crimes which hurt the whole people, China too would soon attain greatness.

Some say that the poverty and weakness of a State have their definite causes, which are four in number, namely (1) the small territory of the country, (2) the poverty of the soil, (3) the small population, (4) the poor talents and capacities of the people.

But in China the area of the country amounts to over 4 million square kilometres, i.e. four times the area occupied by the United States. In respect of wealth hidden in the bowels of the earth, China undoubtedly takes first place in the whole world. In population China also holds the first place. The capacities and talents of the Chinese people have been unequalled since ancient times; moreover, the 5000-year-old culture created by the Chinese is unique, and for thousands of years has been a monument to the capacities of the Chinese people. Thus, of the four chief causes of the poverty and weakness of states, we have not a single one. Why then are we so poor and weak?

To this the reply can be given that only the worthless government of a selfish Government and officials is the reason. And if this virulent ulcer be removed from the body of the Chinese people, undoubtedly China will take its rightful place by the side of other world Powers.

In olden times, in the days of the autocracy, an official was the servant and running-dog of the monarch, but was placed in a position of superiority to the rest of the people, who could do nothing against all his crimes. But now, after the Revolution, the people has become its own master and lord, and the officials should be the servants of the people and be controlled by them. The good elements amongst them should remain, but the worthless should be dismissed. For the people the most important thing is to eliminate all obstacles on its path to development. I repeat that, so soon as we get rid of the elements which are harmful for the State, this will lead to an increase in its well-being, and China will become a powerful and flourishing State.

China is one of the oldest states in the world. Her culture has five thousand years behind it, and, before relations with foreign Powers began, it occupied the first place amongst the Oriental states. The invasion of foreign tribes could not wipe out Chinese customs and ritual. The neighbouring States either expressed their allegiance to China, or sought her friendship and borrowed Chinese culture. *But owing to the fact that China became the leading State, and that the Chinese had before their eyes no example of another state equal to her, conceit, self-satisfaction and arrogance arose. All this entered into our flesh and blood, and we were transformed into a nation apart. We were our own teachers, as in all reconstruction we made use only of our own resources and strength, without resorting to foreign help.*

When a solitary individual is wrecked on a desert island, he has to procure for himself all he requires. He ploughs himself, and consumes as food the fruits of the soil. He spins himself, and wears the yarn he spins, etc. Altogether he carries out the most varied processes of production, and being overloaded with work is unable to commune with his own thoughts. He loses all sense of the meaning of social co-operation. When, in the course of time and for various reasons, this desert island turns out to be on a world shipping route, and it is visited by foreign merchants, they will note the irksome toil of this man and say : " My dear sir, it is quite unnecessary for you to do everything at once, it would be sufficient if you concentrated on one kind of production. This would economise your time and make you master of your own labour." The man, undoubtedly, will not believe them at once, because his state of development will not permit him to do so. He will consider it impossible. The Chinese at the present time in the same way will not believe that China can at one jump raise herself to a high level of power and well-being.

Therefore the self-centredness of China and *her conceited self-satisfaction* have been noted of old. The majority of Chinese cannot understand the benefits of international co-operation, and therefore will not tolerate the thought of any superiority over themselves, or of allowing others to correct their mistakes. This has made China narrow-minded, and undoubtedly has hindered her progress.

Over sixty or seventy years have passed since foreign Powers broke down the Great Wall and came into China, yet Chinese thought still remains that of a solitary man thrown on a desert island. Therefore China is still unable to utilise foreign knowledge and resources to strengthen her own power as a nation.

China as a State possesses colossal territories, incalculable wealth, vast quantities of human energy, and in spite of all resembles a rich old man, who possesses extensive parks, lands and treasures, with a large family, but incapable of keeping house. The lands are deserted and overgrown with weeds, the treasures are kept under lock and key and left without use, while the children and grandchildren are idle, and hunger and cold reign in the house. The house of such an old man gives us the picture of China to-day.

My fellow-countrymen know that our country is moving towards destruction. And if even the animals have a sense of duty to their family and home, man must, without doubt, inwardly feel his duty to help his country. The citizens of China, who not only inhabit our country, but strive that it may be great and flourish, have many ways of bringing this about. I want to set forth one of these possible ways.

I think that we must make use of the circumstance that during the Great War many foreign countries built a large number of factories and generally developed world industry to work up their raw materials. This industry worked almost exclusively for war purposes, and now, with the end of the war, work at many factories must cease. Millions of workers will be thrown out into the streets, and vast sums invested in war industry will earn no profit. The problem of utilising war industry is one of the most serious problems facing Europe, and the best minds of Europe and America are labouring at its solution.

If we are able to take advantage of this occasion, and to utilise the work of these institutions to release the natural riches of China, this, I think, will arouse no opposition from other countries. While for China it will be what the Chinese proverb calls " the heaven-sent opportunity which it is sinful to miss, since to miss it spells disaster." If we miss this opportunity and do not utilise it in the interests of China, in two or three years the European and American factories will return to their pre-war condition, and their development will proceed ten times more rapidly. Once again the world trade war will begin—a war in which our handicrafts and domestic industries, of course, will not be able to compete with their perfected machinery, their colossal scale of operations : and naturally our industry and trade will suffer heavy defeats. But if in the course of the next ten years we carry out a plan for the development of our own industry, with the growth of a heavy machine industry in China we shall be able to avoid this heavy defeat of our industry. Here is a path for the salvation of China !

My fellow-countrymen know that one of the most powerful and mighty states in the world to-day is America : the primary reason for her wealth is the developed state of her industries. We must recall that, at the beginning of the development of her industry, America sought capital in Europe. All her activities at that time bore the character of a risky experiment rather than of the result of a carefully elaborated plan. In addition, in the first days of her development, she did not meet with the favourable circumstance of a stoppage of factories in Europe, such as we have to-day. Her natural riches are less than ours. Yet, despite all this, she developed her industry to an unprecedented extent. To-day she has occupied the first place in world economy.

Let us take, for example, her yearly output of iron and oil. In 1916 her output of iron was 40 million tons, of steel over 43 million tons, while China's output of steel and iron together is about 200,000 tons a year, i.e. $\frac{1}{4}$ per cent. of the American output. America produced 58 million tons of petroleum, 29 million tons of various other combustible oils, and combustible gases in a volume capable of developing 3 million horse-power. Taking all her natural forces together, we can estimate them at approximately 166 million horse-power. If we reckon one horse-power to be equal to the power of eight men, we can reckon that American industry has a reserve of one milliard units of man-power. The population of America is 110 millions. Every man, in addition to his own labour-power, receives in addition 13 units of horse-power to help him, and these 13 units, with their 24 hours of unbroken work, are equivalent to 39 units of man-power (since three shifts of men must be employed in the course of a day). This is the cause of America's wealth.

In China the population is equivalent to 400 millions, of whom 200 millions are capable of working (excluding women and children); but owing to the fact that industry is not developed in our country, and not all can find work for themselves, the numbers working will not amount to over 100 millions, of whom half are employed on unproductive labour. Thus there are only about 50 million people to be found in China engaged in productive labour. And so it turns out that in China, out of eight people, we have only one engaged in productive labour. It is not to be wondered at that our country is poor. The Chinese proverb has it : " One peasant tills the soil, six eat rice," or " the worker works alone, but six people consume the fruits of his labour.''

Compare our position with that of America, where, out of a population of 100 millions, 50 millions are engaged in productive labour, and in addition each has the help of 39 units of man-power. That is why the State there is becoming more wealthy; the growth of productive force exceeds requirements, and this gives America the opportunity to export her surplus abroad, supplying the whole world with her manufactures. These are the causes of the riches or poverty of a people, and these also are the causes of victory or defeat in the world trade war.

Although we seek the way to the quickest possible development of the natural wealth of China, in order to raise her from her state of poverty in the shortest possible time by the extension of her industry, we Chinese do not understand how it is to be done. A man on a desert island will not be able to open up all the mineral wealth of his island, he cannot build roads, establish ports, erect buildings, organise public parks, and in general create a civilised life, even if he live for ten thousand years. He will never be able to carry out such tasks. But if this recluse gets into touch with merchants and foreign visitors, the wealth of the island will be made accessible, and all its affairs will flourish, since the merchants will themselves take care that industry is developed, will make plans, attract capital, and concentrate all their knowledge on securing for themselves as much as possible of the island's wealth. And thereby they will assist in its development.

If a solitary individual cast on a desert island can by the strength of his will complete the task to which he sets his hand, China in her striving to develop her industries must follow the same path. And the question is not whether you will know everything or not, or whether you will be able to realise all your hopes or not, but whether or not you really strive for the object you have set before you.

Speaking of the condition of China and her natural riches, one may say that if at the present time our people is able, as one man, to welcome the influx of foreign capital and foreign knowledge for the development of our industry, then our aim will undoubtedly be achieved in the course of the next ten years. And then the development of our industry will undoubtedly surpass the development of American industry. If there are people who will not believe me in this, I draw their attention to certain facts of the development of American industry.

Ten years ago, when America was planning to construct the Panama Canal, it was thought that the work would be completed in twenty years' time. But when it was carried out, eight years proved to be sufficient. The reason was that technique progressed with extreme rapidity. Moreover, at that time war was declared on Germany, American war industry also progressed very rapidly, and that which, before the war, was calculated to take tens of years was completed in war-time in one year. For example, a year or two had been required previously for building a ship, whereas now it could be built in twenty days. If to-day, with all the technical equipment of war-time at our disposal, we were to begin the cutting of the Panama Canal, only a month would be required to carry this out. Faced with such a development of industrial technique in the European and American countries, my fellow-countrymen should realise all the benefits and necessity of international co-operation, in order, according to the Chinese proverb, to " utilise the superiority of another to remedy your own shortcomings." Going about it in this way, we could hope in the course of a few years for the development of Chinese industry after the manner of the American, which would be very profitable not only for China alone, but would undoubtedly meet the interests of the whole world. That is why there is no foreign scientific expert who does not sympathise with the idea of developing the productive forces of China.

Not so very long ago I presented to all the Governments my work on " a plan for the development of Chinese industry through the medium of international co-operation." I met with great sympathy from the American Government, and I trust that the other Governments also will follow its example in their opinion of my work. Chinese aspirations can be realised only when we understand that, to regenerate the State and to save the country from destruction at this critical moment, we must welcome the influx of large-scale foreign capital on the largest possible scale, and also must consider the question of attracting foreign scientific forces and highly-trained experts to work in our country and train us. Then in the course of the next ten years we shall create our own powerful large-scale industry and shall accumulate technical and scientific knowledge.

After these ten years it will be possible gradually to pay off the foreign loans and acquire complete independence in our work, possessing a complete equipment of the necessary knowledge. Then our national culture can be made literally, the common property of all the Chinese. This will render possible the awakening of the slumbering forces and possibilities of China. Remember the Chinese proverbs: " The day when the river turns blue will never come," " If you lose the right moment, you will always remember it," " When you heal a sick man, always begin with the worst disease," " When saving a man from poverty immediate help is needed," and " Only a man who has been fed and clothed can observe all the ceremonies." If industry is developed, the full development of the economic resources of China is possible, and only then will it be possible to carry out the universal education of the people.

We must seize the moment of the ending of the European war, and the great development of European war industry, to develop our own industry. This can easily be done, and therefore I repeat that " without knowing, one can still achieve."

CHAPTER VII

A PLAN FOR THE DEVELOPMENT OF CHINESE INDUSTRY

IT is calculated that in the last year of the world war the daily expenditure of the various warring peoples amounted roughly to 240 millions of dollars (gold). Let us assume that, with the exercise of the greatest care, only half this sum was spent on military fortifications and other military requirements. This will mean an expenditure of about 120 million gold dollars.

If we look at these military expenses from the commercial standpoint, we see the following picture. The battlefields were the markets for war industry, and the soldiers were the consumers. The war swallowed up everything. Nearly the whole of world industry was militarised. In order to increase the production of munitions, the people of the warring and even of neutral countries were forced to content themselves with the most limited necessaries of life, and to give up, not only articles of luxury, but also their everyday comforts.

Now the war is over, and the market for war industry has closed—let us hope, for ever. To-day the world is faced with the problem of how to organise the post-war economy of Europe. Above we noted that 120 million dollars daily were spent on military supplies. Let us assume that the restoration of European economy will require half this sum, i.e. 60 million dollars : this still leaves us the balance of 60 million dollars daily, which might be utilised for other requirements.

Furthermore, millions of soldiers, who during the war were only consumers, will now once again become a productive force. There has also taken place a concentration and nationalisation of industry which I would call *the second industrial revolution*, and the magnitude of which is much greater than that of the first industrial revolution, in which handicrafts were replaced by machine production. This second industrial revolution will increase the productivity of the worker many times more than the first. Consequently, the concentration and nationalisation of industry on account of the world war will in the future complicate the restoration of post-war industry. Image : a new commerce, created by the war and amounting to 60 million dollars a day or 21 milliard, 900 million dollars a year, must stop as soon as peace is signed. Where in the world can Europe and America find a market to dispose of these enormous supplies remaining after the war ? If these milliards of dollars invested in war industries find no outlet in peace conditions, the world will be faced with an economic crisis. This will not only disturb economic conditions in

Europe and America, but will inflict grave damage on world economy.

The commercial countries of the whole world look on China as a " dumping ground " for their surplus production. Pre-war trade conditions were unfavourable for China. The excess of imports over exports amounted to about 100 million dollars (gold) yearly. The Chinese market could not extend very much in these conditions, since this would have led to the pumping of gold out of China, and would have been profitable only for the foreign countries trading with China. Fortunately, the natural wealth of China is very great, its opening up would create an unlimited market for the whole world, and it could usefully absorb a great part, if not all, of the milliards of dollars remaining in war-time industry.

China is a country in which hand labour still prevails, and which has not yet entered the first stage of industrial evolution, while Europe and America have already reached the second. Therefore China has to begin both periods of industrial evolution at the same time, applying machinery simultaneously with the principle of the nationalisation of industry. In this event China will require machinery for her widespread agriculture ; technical equipment for her rich mines, machinery for her innumerable undertakings of all kinds, for her extensive transport systems, and for all her social needs. How can this new demand for modern machinery affect the reorganisation of war-time industry in Europe and America? The factories which turned out guns can easily be transformed into factories manufacturing steam-rollers for building roads in China. Shops which produced tanks can now make rolling platforms for transporting raw materials from every part of China. All forms of war machinery can be turned into peace-time implements for the general development of the natural wealth of China. The Chinese people will welcome the opening-up of the riches of our country, providing China is protected against the corrupting influence of the mandarins and will have a guarantee of normal intercourse with foreign states.

Some nations of Europe and America may fear that the development of military technique, military organisation, and industrialisation generally will create undesirable competition for foreign industry. I therefore propose a plan for the organisation of a new market in China, sufficiently extensive both to develop China's own productive forces and to absorb the industrial capacity of the foreign Powers. The plan I propose is as follows :

1. The development of systems of communication :
    (a) 100,000 miles of railways.
    (b) 1,000,000 miles of roads.
    (c) Improvement of existing canals :
        (i) Hangchow-Tientsin.
        (ii) Sinkiang-Yangtse.

(*d*) Construction of new canals :
- (i) Liaoyang-Shanghai-kwan.
- (ii) Canals to be planned.

(*e*) Organisation of China's river system :
- (i) Clearing and deepening the bed of the river Yangtse, from Hankow to the sea, in order to permit of ocean-going vessels reaching Hankow.
- (ii) Clearing and deepening the bed of the river Hwangho, to prevent flooding.
- (iii) Clearing the Hsikiang.
- (iv) Clearing the Hwaiho.
- (v) Clearing other rivers.

(*f*) Construction of long-distance telegraph and telephone lines, and also organisation of wireless telegraph stations.

2. The organisation and development of commercial harbours :
- (*a*) The organisation of three large-scale ocean ports, capable of equalling New York in the future, in the north, centre and south of China.
- (*b*) Construction of commercial and fishing harbours along the entire coast.
- (*c*) Construction of commercial docks along all navigable rivers.

3. The building of modern cities, with social

conveniences of all kinds, near all railway centres, principal stations, and harbours.

4. Utilisation of China's waterways.
5. Erection of iron and steel works on the largest scale, and also of cement works to meet building requirements.
6. Development of China's mineral wealth.
7. Development of agriculture.
8. Irrigation work in Mongolia and Chinese Turkestan.
9. Forestry work in central and northern China.
10. The colonisation of Manchuria, Mongolia, Sinkiang, Koko-nor and Tibet.

If the above programme is gradually carried out, China will become, not a mere " dumping-ground " for foreign goods, but a real " economic ocean," capable of absorbing all the surplus capital of the world as rapidly as the industrial countries can produce, in the coming era of the second industrial revolution based on nationalised machine industry. This will eliminate the struggle of commercial competition, not only in China, but throughout the world.

The world war showed mankind that war is destructive both for the victor and for the vanquished, but it is most harmful of all for the attacker. This applies to economic warfare as well as war by force of arms. The American President, Wilson, has proposed the formation of a League of Nations to prevent future wars ; I want to propose the cessation of commercial war by co-operation and mutual aid in the development of China. This will eliminate the chief cause of all future wars.

If my proposal is acceptable to the Powers possessing capital, I shall present further details.

The development of America as an industrial and commercial nation has conferred many benefits on the whole world. The development of China with its 400 million people will create another New World in the economic sense. The nations who take part in the development of China will reap vast benefits. Moreover, international economic co-operation can only assist the strengthening of the ties of friendship between the peoples. Finally, I am certain that in the long run, China will be a foundation-stone of the League of Nations.

For the successful fulfilment of this plan, I propose the following three essential steps. First, that a Board of the Powers supplying capital be organised by agreement, in order to act together and to create an international organisation, with its military organisers, its administrators and its experts in various spheres, to work out plans and standardise materials, thus avoiding trouble and facilitating the works proposed. Secondly, it is essential that the confidence of the Chinese people be secured, in order to serve as a basis for co-operation and for popular support in every way. If these two steps are taken, the third step will be the opening of official negotiations for the conclusion of a final agreement with the Chinese Government relative to the plan put forward.

Finally, the last but most important condition is to prevent the repetition of former mistakes. In 1913 the foreign bankers treated the wishes of the Chinese people with contempt : they thought that they could settle everything with the Chinese Government alone. But it turned out that the treaties which they concluded with the Government, with the help of great bribes, were later refused recognition by the Chinese people. If the foreign banks had chosen a safer road, and had first of all secured the confidence of the Chinese people, and then had begun to negotiate treaties, they would have been more successful.

CHAPTER VIII

THE REVOLUTION IS THE PATH TO THE REGENERA-
TION OF CHINA

*(How the Kuomintang organised the Chinese
Revolution)*

MY appeal for a revolution in China has
been successful, and the destructive part
of the Revolution, in the shape of the
overthrow of the Manchu monarchy, has been
achieved ; but the constructive part has far from
begun. Nevertheless, I do not lose hope in the
successful completion of the Chinese Revolution :
that is why I have devoted to it all my energies.

In the first year of the Republic, when European
writers and scholars were writing thousands of
articles about the Chinese Revolution, and approaching its facts more from the point of view of
morality than of their meaning, I issued the first
chapter of my *Notes on the Chinese Revolution*,
in which I set forth very briefly and concisely
how, twenty years ago, the possibility of a
successful revolution in China was a subject of
great discussion.

Although I lived at the time in London, I could
not name myself as one of the founders of the

" Association for the Regeneration of China."
This at the time involved the risk of persecution.
To-day I restore from memory the contents of
that chapter of my reminiscences, supplementing
them with the facts of the last 30 years, which
formerly I had to omit for conspirative reasons
which will be understood.

From the moment that the idea of revolutionary
struggle awoke within me up to the time of the
foundation of the " Revolutionary League " (out
of which the Kuomintang developed) I was a man
who practised revolution, and therefore all my
revolutionary activities were not very complicated.
I could count on my fingers the names of the
persons who at that time recognised my ideas.
From the time of the foundation of the " Revolutionary League," the work became much more
complicated, and I cannot, of course, recount the
names of all the emigrant patriots, still less of
all the revolutionary heroes at home. I write my
memories as materials for a future historian of
the Kuomintang.

From 1885, i.e. from the time of our defeat in
the war with France, I set before myself the
object of the overthrow of the Tai-Tsing dynasty
and the establishment of a Chinese Republic on
its ruins. At the very beginning I selected for
my propaganda the college at which I was studying, regarding medical science as the kindly aunt
who would bring me out on to the high road of
politics.

Ten years passed like one day. In the Canton Medical School I made friends with Chen-Shi-Liang ; who had a very large circle of acquaintances amongst widely-travelled people who knew China well. When I began talking of revolution, advocating its ideas, he gladly agreed with me, and declared that he would immediately enter a revolutionary Party if I would agree to lead it. After staying a year in the school at Canton, I learned that an English Medical School with a wider programme than that of the Canton School had been opened at Hong Kong. Thereupon, attracted also by the thought that there I should have a wider field for my revolutionary propaganda, I went to Hong Kong to continue my education. For four years I gave up all my time free from studies to the cause of revolutionary propaganda, travelling backwards and forwards between Hong Kong and Amoy. At that time I had scarcely any supporters, with the exception of three persons living in Hong Kong : Chen-Shao-Bo, Yu-Shao-Chi, and Yang-Ho-Lin, and one man at Shanghai, Lu-Ko-Tung. The others avoided me, as a rebel, as they would one stricken with plague.

Living together with my three friends Chen, Yu and Yang, in Hong Kong, we were constantly discussing the revolution. Our thoughts were fixed on the problems of the Chinese Revolution. We studied chiefly the history of revolutions. When it happened that we came together and did not talk of revolution, we did not feel happy.

Thus a few years went by, and we received from our friends the nickname of " the four great and inseparable scoundrels." For me this was a period of revolutionary disputes and preparation.

After finishing school I fixed my attention on two places, Amoy and Yang Chen, nominally for practice, but in reality to begin revolutionary propaganda. At that time Chen-Shi-Liang began recruiting members for the Party. Lu-Ko-Tung and I set out for the North, for Pekin and Tientsin, in order to study how stable the Tai-Tsing dynasty might be, and thence we left for Wuchang to study the situation there.

In 1894 we decided that a suitable moment had arrived, and went to the Philippines to found the " Association for the Regeneration of China," having the intention of establishing connections with Chinese colonists there and receiving help from them. However, we had not realised that the moment was not yet ripe for revolution ; the result of our propaganda in the Philippines was only ten sympathisers, of whom only two brothers, Ten-Yin-Nan and Ten-Teh-Chang, agreed to make considerable sacrifices for our common cause.

This was just at the time when the Imperial armies were suffering one defeat after another. After the loss of Korea, the Monarchy lost the glamour of its power, as before all the Chinese there were clearly revealed the decay and rotten-ness of the Manchu dynasty. Our Shanghai comrade Sun-Yueh-Lo wrote insisting that we return. I, Ten-Yin-Nan and three other comrades returned home for further work, with the intention of organising a revolt at Canton and seizing it.

Our committee was in Hong Kong and our branch at Yang-Chen. There worked at that time in the committee Ten-Yin-Nan, Yang-Tsui-Yun, Haun-Yun-Shan, Chen-Shao-Bo and others, while in the branch at Yang-Chen there were Lu-Ko-Tung, Chen-Shi-Liang, and some instructors from America, and some generals. I often travelled between Canton and Hong Kong. Our tasks by that time were quite well-defined. Preparations were in full blast. We had accumulated considerable strength, and we could by a single blow have effected a great deal. But just at this time the authorities discovered the arms we had smuggled in (500 revolvers), and one of our worthiest comrades, Lu-Ko-Tung, was executed. This was the first sacrifice made by us on the altar of the Chinese revolution. At the same time there were arrested and executed Tse-Hsi and Chu-Gui. About seventy people were arrested, among them the Canton Admiral Tsin-Kui-Guan.

The day of September 9, 1895, I consider to be the day of my first revolutionary defeat. Three days after the defeat I was still in Canton, but ten days later I was forced to escape to Hong Kong by by-roads, and thence left for Japan with comrades Chen-Shi-Liang and Chen-Shao-Bo, intending to land at Yokohama. I cut off my pigtail and put on European clothes, as the date of my return to China was indeterminate. Then I left for the Philippine islands, Chen-Shi-Liang returned to China to restore matters to the point reached before our defeat, while Chen-Shao-Bo remained in Japan to study the political situation. I was introduced at that time to the Japanese Sugawora, and later we made the acquaintance of Sonei and Miasaki, with whom we established connections. This was the beginning of friendly relations between the Chinese revolutionaries and the Japanese.

Having arrived in the Philippines, I began to gather comrades to strengthen our " Association for the Regeneration of China," but even old comrades, owing to our defeat, did not conceal their despair, while some simply forswore our ideas. Owing to the absence of the necessary factors for the development of a revolutionary movement, the latter slowed down somewhat. There was no reason why I should stay long in the Philippines, and I decided to leave for America, in order to establish connections with the organisation of Chinese emigrants there.

The day of my departure was fixed, and I was walking outside the town when I met a carriage, in which I recognised my teacher Kandeli and his wife. I jumped on to the foot-board, to their great surprise and even fear, as they apparently took me for an evilly-disposed person. They did not recognise me, as I had considerably altered my appearance. When I said, " I am Sun-Yat-

Sen," they burst out laughing and began shaking me by the hand. I asked them how they came there. They explained that they were on their way home, and were spending the day here taking advantage of the boats stopping there. I offered them my services as guide, which they accepted. At the end of the day, I told them that I should shortly be undertaking a trip round the world, and hope to be in London also, on my way to America. With this we parted, after friendly greetings.

Amongst the Chinese emigrants in America I found an even more sleepy atmosphere then in the Philippines. I crossed the continent from San-Francisco to New York. On my way I stopped at various places for a few days—for ten days at the most—everywhere preaching that to save our mother-country from threatening destruction we must overthrow the Tai-Tsing dynasty, and that the duty of every Chinese citizen was to help to reconstruct China on a new democratic basis.

Although I spared no effort in this propaganda, the people to whom it was directed remained apathetic and little responsive to the ideas of the Chinese Revolution. At that time, however, there were fairly widespread amongst the Chinese emigrants the so-called "Hung-Men" societies, although by my time they had been reduced to little more than mutual aid clubs. Their history is as follows. The supporters of the Ming dynasty[1]

---

[1] Overthrown by the Manchu Tai-Tsing dynasty in 1644.

raised several rebellions against the Tai-Tsing dynasty, but always suffered defeat at the hands of the Imperial troops, and when, during the rule of Kan-Si, the Manchu dynasty reached the height of its strength, all the efforts of the supporters of the Ming dynasty proved to be doomed to failure. Some of them paid for their audacity with their lives, others managed to escape. Seeing the impossibility of overthrowing the Tai-Tsings, they seized then on the idea of nationalism and began preaching it, handing it down from generation to generation. Their main object in organising the " Hung-Men " societies was the overthrow of the Tai-Tsing dynasty and the restoration of the Ming dynasty. The idea of nationalism was for them an auxiliary. They carried on all their affairs in profound secret, avoiding Government officials and hiding also from the Chinese intellectuals, whom they looked upon as the eyes and ears of the Chinese Government. Knowing the psychology of the masses, the " Hung-Men " societies spread their nationalist ideas by means of various plays, which had a great effect amongst the people. In the ideas they spread abroad, everything was based on arousing discontent with one's position and with existing inequality, and preaching the necessity for revenge. Their passwords and watchwords were dirty and vulgar phrases, and Chinese intellectuals avoided them in disgust.

Party solidarity, which afforded them help

when in trouble, and a certain co-ordination in their activities, proved very helpful for wanderers and for various Chinese prodigal sons. Their nationalist ideas helped them in their struggle against the hated Tai-Tsing dynasty, and consequently fed their hopes of a restoration of the Ming dynasty.

The Chinese people were in constant conflict with the Imperial officials, and never abandoned their opposition to the Tsing dynasty. The watchwords : " Down with Tsing ! " and " Long live Ming ! " were near and dear to many Chinese. But the same cannot be said of our overseas emigrants, as they, being abroad in a free country, had no necessity to organise societies of a fighting character. Therefore in America the " Hung-Men " societies naturally lost their political colour, and became benefit clubs. Many members of the " Hung-Men " societies did not rightly understand the meaning and exact aims which their society pursued. When I approached them, during my stay in America, and asked them, why did they want to overthrow the Tsing dynasty and restore the Ming dynasty, very many were not able to give me any positive reply. Later, when our comrades had carried on a protracted revolutionary propaganda in America for several years, members of the " Hung-Men " societies at last realised they were old nationalist revolutionaries.

Although my stay in America was of little importance for the further destinies of the Chinese

Revolution, it nevertheless aroused fears and misgivings on the part of the Imperial Government. Therefore on my arrival in London I almost fell into the clutches of the Imperial Embassy, but I was saved from peril by my teacher Kandeli. It was owing to him that I was saved from the great danger which threatened me.

After escaping from London, I went to Europe to study the methods of its political administration, and also to make the acquaintance of representatives of the Opposition parties. In Europe I understood that, although the foremost European countries had achieved power and popular government, they could not accord complete happiness to their peoples. Therefore the leading European revolutionaries strive for a social revolution, and I conceived the idea of the simultaneous settlement, by means of the revolution, of the questions of national economy, national independence, and popular freedom. Hence arose my so-called " san-min-chu," or the idea of democracy based on three principles.

The revolution was my principal aim in life, and therefore I hastened to conclude my business in Europe, in order not to lose time dear to the revolution. I left for Japan, considering that there, nearer to China, we could more successfully carry out our revolutionary plans. On my arrival in Japan I was met at Yokohama by two leaders of the Japanese Popular Party. Later on we met in Tokio like old friends, and discussed all questions affecting China with great frankness. Just at that time the Japanese Popular Party came to power, and Okuma was appointed Minister for Foreign Affairs. I was introduced to him and to other Japanese politicians. This was our first contact with representatives of Japanese ruling circles. Then I met Soezima and other representatives of the Japanese Opposition.

Later they all greatly helped the cause of the Chinese Revolution.

There were fully ten thousand Chinese emigrants in Japan, but an atmosphere of inertia prevailed amongst them. They were terribly afraid of the idea of revolution, just like the Chinese emigrants in other countries. Our comrades had worked amongst them for some years, yet it turned out that only a hundred odd had joined the revolutionary movement, which did not represent one per cent. of our emigrants in Japan. While the propaganda of revolutionary ideas amongst the emigrants was so difficult and thankless, it was even more difficult in China. The Chinese were not repelled by the idea of overthrowing the Manchu dynasty, and willingly entered our Party ; but their intelligence was very weak, there was little solidarity amongst them, and they had no convictions. They could be used as a passive force, but under no circumstances could they be an active force.

From 1895, i.e. from the moment of our first defeat, until 1900, five years went by, which were a period of great difficulty and suffering for the Chinese revolutionary movement. The revolutionary foundation we had built up in the course of ten years, both in the sense of the work of each of our comrades and in the sense of the positions we had secured, was destroyed. Propaganda abroad also had little success. At this time, too, monarchist organisations grew up and became very active on the political arena. Our hopes were almost destroyed, but our comrades did not fall into despair and courageously looked ahead.

I sent Chen-Shao-Bo to Hong Kong to publish a paper there for the spreading of revolutionary ideas, and ordered Li-Kiang-Jo to proceed to the province of Chekiang to organise the forces there. I instructed Chen-Shi-Liang to proceed to Hong Kong to establish an organising bureau there, and recruit new members for our Party.

Very soon there took place the amalgamation of the " Association for the Regeneration of China " with organisations which had sprung up in the Kwantung province and other provincial organisations of the Yangtse valley.

At this time also there took place the movement inspired by the Manchu dynasty which was known as the " Boxer Rebellion." Eight foreign Powers despatched their troops to China and opened military activities. I decided that this moment ought not to be lost, and instructed Chen-Shi-Liang to leave for Huchow, in order to organise a rising there, and despatched Li-Kiang-Jo to Yangchen for the same purpose. While all these preparations were going on very feverishly, I went to Hong Kong with some foreign officers, intending to get across to my native country by water, there to assume personal control over the best forces of the nation, and to organise a disciplined revolutionary army to save China from destruction. But quite unexpectedly for myself I was betrayed by some scoundrel, and the Hong Kong authorities subjected me to a search and would not allow me to land. In this way I was not able to carry out my original plan. Therefore, I placed full responsibility at Huchow on Chen-Shi-Liang, and sent Yang-Tsu-Ya, Yun-Li-Tsi, Chen-Shao-Bo and others to Hong Kong to help him. I returned myself to Japan, whence, I travelled to Formosa, intending again to think out some means of getting into China. The Governor-General of Formosa was, at that time, Kodama, a man who sympathised a great deal with the Chinese Revolution, as he considered that the North was entirely in the grip of anarchy. He instructed one of his assistants to enter into negotiations with me, promising that if there were a serious outbreak he would support us.

I extended our original plan, increasing the number of specialist officers, as at that time our party had too few politically conscious military experts at its disposal. On the other hand, I ordered Chen-Shi-Liang to alter the original plan of attacking the principal city of the province, and instead to seize the maritime area and concentrate our forces there, and then to begin the attack.

Chen-Shi-Liang immediately left for the appointed place on receipt of my instructions. With for the most part peasant detachments under his command, he attacked the Imperial soldiers at Sinyang and Shenchuan and disarmed them, and then attacked Lungan, Tanshui-Yunhu, and other points. Everywhere he was successful, with the result that the Imperial troops began to disperse as soon as they came into contact with his advance guards. He then occupied successively the whole maritime area from Sinyang to Huchow, and there awaited my arrival with our supporters, and also the arrival of arms and military equipment. However, quite unexpectedly for us, ten days after our revolutionary armies opened the attack, there were changes in the Japanese Government, and the new Premier took up an attitude towards China which was quite the opposite of his predecessor's. He forbade any negotiations between the Governor-General of Formosa and the Chinese revolutionaries, and also prohibited both the export of arms and the entry of Japanese officers into the Chinese Revolutionary Army. This disarranged my whole plan. I sent Yamada and a few more comrades to the camp of Chen-Shi-Liang, to inform him of what had taken place and to instruct him to act according to the circumstances of the moment. When they arrived at his camp, thirty days had passed since the beginning of operations. An army of 10,000 men had been collected with was impatiently awaiting the arrival of arms and superior officers.

When they received Yamada's information, it was decided immediately to dissolve the troops, and Chen-Shi-Liang returned to Hong Kong with some hundreds of our comrades. Yamada lost his way, was seized by the Imperial troops, and was executed. This was the first foreigner who sacrificed his life on the altar of the Chinese Revolution.

At the time that Chen-Shi-Liang was in the thick of the fight, Li-Kiang-Jo at Canton attempted to help him, but unsuccessfully. Then he decided to throw a bomb into the office of the Governor of the two Kwan provinces (Kwantung and Kwangsi), but the bomb did not burst, and he was arrested and executed. This was the second hero to perish for the Republic. He was a man with a strong will wise and sincere : he might be compared with Lu-Ko-Tung, as their courage and their talents resembled one another. They both painted and wrote verses well. Lu-Ko-Tung was courageous and Li-Kiang-Jo was fearless, and it was truly sad that owing to our defeat we lost these two most worthy men of their age. The loss of these two heroes was undoubtedly unfortunate for the future of the Chinese Revolution, but the spiritual strength and courage of these two comrades who perished were worthy of the imitation of all those who remained alive. I always remember them: although they are dead, yet "their souls still continue to dwell around my breast."

The 1900 affair was the second defeat of the Chinese Revolution. However, after this defeat the attitude of the Chinese people towards us changed greatly. After our first defeat, all looked on us as rioters, robbers, who were doing something unjust. We were overwhelmed with curses and abuse, we were looked upon as poisonous snakes, and people avoided our acquaintance. After the defeat of 1900, although the former voices which cursed us were heard as loudly as ever, there were already many intelligent Chinese who regretted our defeat and expressed to us their sympathy. If this be compared with the past, of course we shall find a vast difference, and our comrades who realised this were greatly delighted in their hearts at these signs of China's gradual awakening from sleep. The glamour of the power of the Tai-Tsing dynasty was finally dispersed when the troops of the eight Powers entered as conquerors into Pekin, while the representatives of the Imperial House fled, and after an armistice agreed to an indemnity for damages of 100 millions. The material conditions of the Chinese people grew worse and worse, and a terrible peril continued to hang over our Motherland. All intelligent Chinese began to understand that China was on the brink of destruction. From this moment a new revolutionary wave began to grow up.

At this time nearly all the provinces began to send students to Japan to receive their education there. Amongst the students who came to Tokyo there turned out to be many people with young and clear heads. They seized on revolutionary ideas at once, and soon entered the revolutionary movement. All the arguments of the students of that day, and all their thoughts, turned around revolutionary questions. At a students' New Year's Day meeting Lu-Chen-Yui made a big speech on a revolution to overthrow the Manchu dynasty. He was expelled from the University at the demand of the Imperial Minister in Tokyo. Other students, such as Tsi-Yuan-Chen, Chen-Cha-Chai, Chai-Bo-Tsuan, published popular newspapers to spread revolutionary ideas.

This revolutionary movement amongst the Chinese students found its way into China. At Shanghai the students Chang-Tai-Yang, Wu-Wei-Hoi, Cho-Chang and others utilised the Christian papers for revolutionary propaganda. Their actions were complained of by representatives of the Imperial authorities, in consequence of which they were arrested and imprisoned on the territory of the foreign concession. One of them, however, managed to escape abroad. Then there followed the only trial of its kind, in which the dynasty brought an action against an individual in the foreign Court, and won its case. Cho-Chang was sentenced only to two years' imprisonment.

During this period the popular movement grew

stronger and stronger. The emigrants hailed with joy the appearance of Cho-Chang's book, *The Revolutionary Army,* in which he attacked the Tai-Tsing dynasty very strongly. It played a big part in the revolutionary movement amongst the Chinese emigrants. This period I consider to be the beginning of the epoch of the wide development of the Chinese revolutionary movement.

In 1900–1903 the Governor of Annam several times requested the French Consul at Tokyo to invite me to meet him personally, but somehow I could not find the time for this. When the Exhibition was opened at Hanoi I went there, but when I arrived in Annam I learned that the Governor had resigned and left for home, instructing his Chief Secretary to receive me well. During my stay at Hanoi I made the acquaintance of Hua-Lun-Chen, Wang-Tsei-Ting, Wa-Bi-Yang and other comrades : all of them later became our sympathisers, and took a great part in the affair at Kiang Liang. At the end of the Hanoi Exhibition, I again left for a journey round the world through Japan and America.

When travelling through Japan I was met by Lo-Chung-Kai, Fu-Fu-Ma and others, who expressed their full sympathy with the Revolution. I requested them to set up an organisation amongst the most intelligent comrades. Later on, when our " United League " was being set up, they brought very many people with them. After the defeat at Huchow, in the period before the setting up of the " United League " we were joined by Li-Tsi-Tang and Hun-Tsuan-Fu at Canton and Huan-Ki-Tsiang and Ma-Fu-Yi in the province of Hunan. The revolutionary movement in China was growing much stronger. The emigrants who lived abroad were gradually being inclined to the side of the Revolution by the revolutionary propaganda of the students and the popular movement in China, and during my journey across Japan everywhere expressed their sympathy to me.

In the Spring of 1905 I arrived in Europe once again, and the majority of the students there were supporters of the Revolution. They had only just arrived in Europe from Japan or China. The revolutionary wave seized on them, and they soon began to go on from arguments about the Revolution to direct revolutionary activities. I then set forth my long-guarded ideas about democracy embodied in three principles and the " Fivefold Constitution," in order to create a revolutionary organisation on their basis. Our first meeting took place at Brussels, and thirty people entered our League. The second meeting was organised in Berlin, and there twenty odd persons joined. The third meeting was in Paris, where ten people entered the League ; but at the fourth meeting in Tokyo several hundred new members joined. There were in our League representatives of all the provinces of China, with the exception of Kansu, as Kansu had not yet sent any students to Japan. At the time our League was being set up the word " revolution " was still terrifying, and therefore our League was simply called the " United League," which name it retained for fairly long.

After the creation of the " United League," I began to believe that a new era of the Chinese Revolution was opening before us. Previously, I had more than once met with great difficulties, I had been spat upon and ridiculed by all. I more than once suffered defeats, but I audaciously moved forward, although I must confess that I did not dream of the accomplishment of the overthrow of the Manchu dynasty still in my life-time. However, from the Autumn of 1905 onwards, after the creation of the revolutionary " United League," I became convinced that the great cause of the Chinese Revolution would be accomplished during my lifetime. It was then that I decided to put forward the watchword of a Chinese Republic, and to advocate it before all the members of our Party, in order that when they returned home each to his own province they should widely support the necessity of revolution to set up a Republic. Scarcely a year had passed before 10,000 people joined our " United League." Branches were organised in almost all of the provinces, and from this time forward the revolutionary movement went ahead with great strides. Its further development exceeded all my anticipations.

The foreign governments at that time also began to look upon the Chinese revolutionaries favourably. On one occasion when I was passing through Woosung on my way to Japan, I was visited by a French officer, on the instructions of his superior officers, who informed me that his Government intended to support the Chinese Revolution, and then asked me what was the position as regards the revolutionary forces. I told him the true state of affairs. Then he again asked me how matters stood with the organisation of our military forces in the provinces, and our connections with the districts, adding that if all were not well in this respect his Government would immediately give us help. To this I replied that in this respect all had not yet been done, and asked him to send us agents to help us, and also to investigate the position and establish connections. They then sent some officers from their Tientsin staff to be at my disposal.

I instructed Lo-Chung-Kai to organise an office at Tientsin, instructed Li-Chung-Sha with some officers to leave for Kwantung and Kwangsi to investigate the position, ordered Hu-Yi-Chen to travel with some officers to the provinces of Szechuan and Yunnan and also to investigate the local position, and finally ordered Kiao-Yi-Chai to travel with some officers to Nankin and Wuhan for the same purpose. At that time there were freshly mobilised troops at Nanking and Wuhan, and they welcomed our comrades on their arrival. At Nanking preliminary negotiations with them were carried on by a certain comrade Chao-Po. He had conferences and secret meetings with their officers up to the rank of battalion commander. At Wuhan, Lu-Tsia-Yun carried on negotiations. Together with some of the military comrades, he summoned a general meeting in a church, to which very many people came : it is said that there was even present the Commander of the troops, Chang-Hu. At this meeting all present made speeches entirely in favour of the revolution, and the French officers also supported this.

All this became widely known, and soon afterwards Chang-Chi-Tung, the Governor-General of the provinces of Hupeh and Kwantung, sent a foreigner, who worked in the Customs, to spy on the French officers. By expressing his loyalty to the Chinese Revolution, this spy entered into close relations with the French officers. They accepted him as a European, and told him everything. Chang-Chi-Tung then sent reports to the Imperial Government at Pekin, informing them of all the plans of the Chinese revolutionaries, both real and invented. The Imperial Government when it received these reports, immediately opened negotiations with the French Embassy on this question. The French Embassy, not being acquainted with all the circumstances, asked its Government what should be done with the officer referred to, to which it received a reply instructing it to hush up the whole affair. The Pekin authorities could do nothing. Some time later, however, the French Government was changed, and the new Cabinet took quite a different view of the question. It recalled this officer and others, and subsequently Lu-Tsia-Yun was arrested and executed.

From the very foundation of the "United League" we published newspapers which spread far and wide the ideas of the Chinese Revolution, democracy embodied in the three principles and the "Fivefold Constitution." A wave of revolutionary thought rolled all over China, but it reached its highest point when we began to publish journals. At that time we were joined by famous heroes like Hsu-Si-Lin, Sun-Yaen-Tsi, Tsu-Tsin and others.

The revolt at Pinli began in 1907, and was carried out independently by our "United League" with its own forces, the revolutionary army being organised out of its members. At the time that our revolutionary army was conducting a life-and-death struggle with the Imperial troops at Pinli, all our Tokyo members were yearning to go, and besieged our Committee with requests to send them to the front to take part in the fighting. I know of cases when some comrades who were not able to leave for the front cried like children.

Unfortunately, we were not informed in good time about the revolt at Pinli, which was begun by members of our League, and we learned of it so late that we were unable to make adequate preparation. We lost the battle at Pinli and Lu-Tao-Yi, Nin-Tiao-Yi, Yuan-Hun-Yin and other comrades were captured by the Imperial troops. Part were executed, and part sentenced to imprisonment. This was the first battle-christening of the members of our " United League." After this it could be said that the revolutionary movement seized on the whole country in unprecedented dimensions. The members of our League in Tokyo, of course, could also not remain passive spectators. Then the Imperial Government proposed to the Japanese Government that we should be expelled from the borders of Japan.

I set out from Japan with Han-Min and Ching-Wei for Annam, in order to organise our office at Hanoi, with a view to a new insurrection. We raised a revolt at Chaochow : however, the troops of Huan-Kan were defeated there. This was our third defeat. Then followed the revolt of Min-Tan at Huchow, but this also suffered defeat. This was my fourth defeat. In the districts of Lian and Tsian a rising took place on account of unwillingness to pay taxes. The Imperial Government sent 4000 of its troops, under the leadership of Kuo-Jen-Chang and Chao-Po-Siang to restore order. I ordered Huang-Kai-Tsiang and Hu-Yi-Chen to visit their respective camps and persuade them to go over to the side of the revolution. Both generals declared that if a real revolutionary army actually revolted, they would join it.

After this we sent organisers to the Lian and Tsien districts to mobilise all the groups of intelligent citizens and co-ordinate their activity. We also sent Suan-E— and Chuan-Chi to buy arms in Japan. Moreover, we collected comrades in Annam, and invited many French officers from amongst those demobilised as instructors. We considered that, once we had arms, we would be able to seize the whole maritime area from Fanchen to Tungsin. Tungsin is extremely suitable for the organisation of a revolutionary army, as it borders on the French concession, and various kinds of military equipment can be transported with great convenience over the river which separates them.

With the arrival of arms we reckoned on equipping and arming 2000 odd men, then to collect an army of 6000 men in the Tsien district, and only then to convince Kuo-Jen-Chang to come over to our side. In this way we hoped to organise a strong army, which after a short period of training could easily occupy the provinces of Kwantung and Kwangsi, and then advance towards the Yangtse and join the lately mobilised troops of Nanking and Wuhan, which would give us at last sufficient forces for the successful completion of the revolution. However, quite unexpectedly for us, some troubles took place in our Tokyo committee, and the plan for the purchase of arms fell through. Fanchen at this time was attacked, but as the arms did not arrive, I lost confidence in the comrades who had set out to procure them, while those who had attacked Fanchen, seeing that the arms still did not arrive, withdrew to Kiangchow, hoping that the troops of Kuo-Jen-Chang would join them. The latter, however, seeing that our forces were too weak, could not make up his mind to help us, fearing that he himself would be crushed by the Imperial troops which had been despatched as reinforcements. Our troops then retreated to Linshan, expecting to be helped there by the troops of Chao-Po-Siang : but the latter, seeing that Kuo-Jen-Chang was not moving, also did not dare to move. Thereupon our army, in view of its weakness, decided to retreat to Shi-Wan-Dashan, which was done. This was our fifth defeat.

After our plan of insurrection was defeated in the districts of Tsian and Lian, I personally took the lead of Comrades Huang-Kai-Tsiang, Hu-Han-Min, some French officers and 100 other comrades, and by a sudden attack seized three forts at Chen-Nan-Kwang, and took into our ranks the soldiers who surrendered. Here I hoped to collect also the comrades who had retreated to Shi-Wan-Dashan, and by our joint efforts to attack Huchow. But I did not then reckon with the fact that the comrades at Shi-Wan-Dashan were too far away. We, a group of about 100 men, with the three guns we had captured, fought for seven days against the thousands of men led by Lu-Tsi-Kwang and Lu-Yin-Tin, and then retreated to Annam. While I was passing through

Lianshan, I was recognised by a spy of the Imperial authorities, who approached the French Government, with the result that I was expelled from Hanoi. This was our sixth defeat.

After my departure from Hanoi, I gave instructions for all preparations to be made for a new invasion of the Lian and Tsian districts. At the same time I ordered Huang-Min-Tang to seize Hokow, for the purpose of advancing further into the Province of Yunnan and establishing our base there. Shortly afterwards Huang-Kai-Tsiang moved out of Annam with his friends and marched into the districts mentioned, where he fought for several months, bringing panic on the Imperial troops and acquiring thereby great repute. However, after some time he also retreated, owing to lack of military equipment and lack of support. This I consider our seventh defeat.

After my arrival in Sinchow—in about a month —Huang-Min-Tang with his 100 comrades seized Hokow, shot the principal officers, won over 1000 soldiers who surrendered, and began to await instructions from our committee. At that time I was in Nanyang, and could not cross French territory to take command personally at the front, and therefore instructed Huang-Kai-Tsiang to assume the command himself. Huang-Kai-Tsiang was already half-way there, when he unexpectedly fell under the suspicion of the French authorities, and was taken to Hanoi, where, after communication with the Chinese

Government, he was forbidden to enter China. The insurgents at Hokow were thus left without a leader, as a result of which we lost the moment suitable for an offensive. Huang-Min-Tang held out for over a month, fighting continuously all the time, but the enemy were ten times his numbers and we did not succeed in retaining Hokow. Finally the detachments of Huang-Min-Tang, numbering 600 men, withdrew to Annam, which was our eighth defeat.

In consequence of the insistence of the Pekin Government, our comrades were expelled from the French possessions and went to Singapore, but were stopped there by the British officials, who would not allow them to land. Then the French Consul in Singapore entered into negotiations with the Governor-General, stating that these were 600 Chinese revolutionaries, who had retreated after their defeat on to French territory, and in consequence of their own wishes had been sent to Singapore. The Governor-General of Singapore replied that he did not recognise Chinese who fought against their own Government as belligerents, and that he considered them to be not political criminals but pure rebels, and therefore they would not be allowed to land. However, after two days' delay in the port, the French succeeded in carrying their point, and our comrades were permitted to land. During the revolutionary fighting at Hokow the French Government had observed neutrality, but in

done

effect it had even then recognised the revolutionaries as a belligerent side, and therefore it could not treat the comrades sent to Singapore as mutineers pure and simple.

After this last defeat, comrade Ching-Wei was very depressed, and decided to leave for Pekin to carry out terrorist acts: after consulting with me, he left for Pekin with a few comrades; but the attempt he made failed, and he was thrown into prison together with Huang-Fu-Chen. They were set free only after the Wuhan rising.

Up to the creation of our " United League," there were very few people who helped the revolutionary army in money, and those only from amongst my personal friends. No one else dared to help us. After the creation of our " United League " we began to be helped from outside. Of those who helped us most at that time, I can mention Chang-Tsin-Tsiang, who sold his factory in Paris and gave us a sum of 60 or 70 thousand dollars. Further, amongst the number of the most generous subscribers, I will mention Huang-Tsin-Nan of Annam, who gave us all his savings, amounting to several thousand dollars. I can also mention several rich merchants of Annam—Li-Cho-Fong, Tseng-Hsi-Chow and Ma-Pei-Chen—who subscribed some tens of thousands of dollars.

After my repeated defeats, I could not live freely either in Japan, Hong Kong, or Annam, or generally in the districts bordering on China. Thus work within the boundaries of my native country was almost impossible for me. Therefore, entrusting the leadership to comrades Huang-Kai-Tsiang and Hu-Han-Min, I myself once more set out on a journey round the world, with the special purpose of collecting resources for the Chinese Revolution.

Subsequently, comrades Huang-Tsiang and Hu-Han-Min organised at Hong Kong a " Chief Committee for Southern Affairs," and, together with comrades Chao-Po-Tsiang, Ni-Yang-Chen, Chu-Chi-Sin and Chen-Chiung-Min, raised a rebellion of the newly-mobilised troops in the province of Kwantung. This movement was well thought out, and the banner of insurrection was raised in 1910.

Comrade Ni-Yan-Tiang went to the camp of the insurgents and assumed leadership of the revolt. From Shaho they moved on the chief city of the province, and had already reached Han-Chi-Gan, but there met the Government troops, and by an accidental explosion Ni-Yang-Tiang was killed. Left without a leader, the rebels dispersed in various directions. This was our ninth defeat.

At this time I was leaving America for the East. When I arrived in San Francisco I learned of the revolt. I immediately set sail for the Philippine Islands and Japan with the object of returning to China. But in Yokohama I was recognised by spies and could not remain there, and left for the South, where I decided to meet Huang-Kai-

Tsiang and Hu-Han-Min to confer on the plan of our further activities. Amongst the comrades at this time there was great depression. After our defeat and the destruction of our strongest committee, we had lost advantageous positions. Most of our fighters were forced to flee and emigrate. We had not sufficient strength to organise all anew. Therefore the comrades were in an extremely pessimistic frame of mind, and when we began to talk of our future plans, they all sighed heavily and did not look one another in the eyes. I took the floor, and began to tell them that our defeats in the past were much heavier. Our detachments at the present time might be few, but the revolutionary wave was growing and broadening day by day, and the spirit of the Chinese was rising. "And if we now turn our attention to the plan I proposed and do not lose heart, I promise to find the resources for future work." They replied : " If we have not the resources necessary to satisfy our own needs as emigrants, how can we find resources for the Revolution ? "

I replied again that I would find the resources. Then comrade Bo declared that if we were really to begin action again we must immediately send a comrade with several thousand dollars to the Province of Szechuan, to help the comrades there and prevent their dispersal. Only then will it be possible to think of setting up a new committee and again reopening the struggle. " We must," said comrade Bo, " return to Hong Kong for a full discussion, and also immediately send five thousand dollars to Szechuan. But if we intend further action, we require several tens of thousands of dollars."

I then summoned the Chinese emigrants who sympathised with us for a conference, the result of which was that they collected eight thousand dollars for us, and in addition decided to delegate comrades to collect the sum we required in the various regions and provinces. In the space of a few days we collected sixty or seventy thousand dollars.

We worked out a plan of action. I went to the Dutch possession, but was not admitted, and was also refused a passage through the British possessions ; so that I had nothing else left but once again to leave for Europe or America. I went to America, where I travelled from corner to corner, agitating amongst the Chinese emigrants and urging them to help us and to subscribe money for the cause of the Revolution. On this occasion there were very many sympathisers amongst the emigrants in America.

At this time took place the Kwantung rising. All the most heroic revolutionaries took part, and although we once again suffered defeat, the glorious deeds of the seventy-two heroes resounded throughout the world. This was our tenth defeat.

Even before the rising, comrades Chen-Yin-Shin, Sun-Tun-Chu, Tan-Shi-Bin, Tsui-Tsiao-Shen and others, seeing that in the province of Kwantung we were suffering one defeat after another decided to transfer the centre of their attention to Hankow, Wuchang and Hanyang, i.e. to work amongst the garrisons there, consisting as they did of newly-mobilised soldiers. After some agitation had gone on amongst them, their state of mind was so revolutionary that the Governor-General of the Hupeh and Kwantung provinces ordered the most revolutionary units to be transferred to the province of Szechuan. However, after the last Kwantung rising, the number of supporters of the Revolution began to increase daily. The Imperial authorities of the Tsing dynasty were in a state of panic terror, fearing most of all a blow from Wuchang, and therefore the Governor-General of the above-mentioned provinces, Jui-Chen, made an agreement with the Consul of a " certain " state that, when the revolutionaries rise in revolt, he must land his troops and bombard the city.

The atmosphere in Wuchang was electrical. Comrades Sun-Wu, Liu, and others decided to act and raise a rebellion of the troops. However, quite unexpectedly, our committee was discovered, and thirty people were imprisoned ; but Hi-Yin-Shan, while in the prison at Wuchang, succeeded in notifying Chen-Yin-Shin and giving him warning, so that he should not too fall into the trap. At this time, there fell into the hands of the Imperial authorities a list of our artillerymen and other soldiers who were taking part in the work of the

Revolution. With the object of saving these comrades from inevitable destruction, it was necessary to act immediately with great urgency. Therefore, Sun-Bi-Chen first went into action, followed by Tsao-Tsi-Min and others. At the head of their detachments they attacked the Governor-General's office and began bombarding it.

Governor Jui-Chen, hearing the noise of the cannonade, immediately fled to Hankow, and appealed to the Consul of a "certain" country to bombard the city. But according to the Treaty of 1900, no country had the right of independent action in China, and therefore a meeting of the Consular body was summoned to discuss the question of whether the city should be bombarded to restore order. It turned out that the Consuls had no definite opinion. They were then addressed by my old acquaintance, the French Consul, who informed the meeting that this rising had taken place on my instructions, and declared that the revolutionaries of the Sun-Yat-Sen Party were by no means making a senseless mutiny, but were fighting for the reconstruction of political authority. Therefore, they cannot be classed with the Boxers, and they should not be interfered with. The senior member of the Consular body at that time was the Russian, and he took up the same position as the French Consul. The other Consuls joined with them, and passed a resolution of non-intervention and maintenance of neutrality.

Seeing that the Consul was not acting according to the Agreement, and that he could not be relied upon, Jui-Chen fled to Shanghai. But as soon as the Governor-General fled, Chang-Hu followed him. In this way the Imperial authorities eliminated themselves.

Amongst the revolutionaries, during this time, Sun-Wu was wounded, while the Shanghai comrades had not arrived. Tsa-Tsi-Min, Chang-Chen and other members of the " United League " then forced Colonel Li-Yuan-Hung to assume the Governor-Generalship of the Hupeh province, and only then was order gradually restored.

The first revolutionary outbreak thus took place in the provinces of Hunan and Hupeh, but unity of action was not established between them. Our success at Wuchang was due in great measure to the flight of Jui-Chen, since, if he had not fled, Chang-Hu would not have fled also, and then the troops subordinated to him undoubtedly would not have mutinied. The majority of the mobilised soldiers at Wuchang were on the side of the Revolution : but most of them were transferred earlier to the province of Szechuan. Of the troops who remained in Wuchang there were only the artillerymen and the engineering troops, but they would have sold their lives dearly if their officers had not fled. And so, " Heaven itself helped China."

The object of our Revolution, of course, was not limited to the capture of Wuchang alone. The comrades began to display activity throughout the country. Very rapidly we seized fifteen provinces. Earliest of all Shanghai went over to us, immediately after the fall of Hankow. Chen-Yin-Shin was acting there, and immediately after Shanghai he seized Nanking. Thus the seizure of Wuchang, Hankow and Hanyang gave us the keys to the whole of Central China, while Chen-Yin-Shin at Shanghai was also growing in strength.

While the rising was taking place at Wuchang, I arrived in Columbia. Ten days before my arrival there, I received a telegram from Huan-Kai-Tsiang from Hong Kong, but as the cipher was in my baggage, I could not read the telegram, and only deciphered it when I arrived in one of the towns of the State of Columbia. The telegram stated that Tsui-Chen had arrived at Hong Kong and reported that money was necessary to assist the rising of the recently mobilised soldiers. Being in Columbia, I had not any money, of course, and could not procure it, and intended to send a telegram postponing the rising. But night fell, and, being tired by my journey, I postponed it till the morning, in order to think over the question again with a clear head. I woke up the next morning at 11 o'clock and, being hungry, went out to a restaurant. On my way I bought a newspaper and, arriving at the restaurant, un-folded it ; immediately my eyes were met by a telegram about the capture of Wuchang by the revolutionary troops. I thereupon sent a detailed telegram to Huan-Kai-Tsiang, in which I explained the reason for my silence.

In twenty days I could come to Shanghai and take a personal part in the revolutionary struggle, but for us our diplomatic front was more important even than the military front for the moment. Therefore, I decided to concentrate my efforts on diplomatic affairs, and only after settling this business to return home.

The state of affairs at that time was as follows. America had proclaimed in respect of China the principle of the open door and the maintenance of its sovereignty, but in relation to the Revolution America had no definite opinion. However, American public opinion took our side. So far as the French Government and French people were concerned, our Revolution met with sympathy. In England public opinion expressed its sympathy with the Revolution, but the Government was opposed to it. Germany and Russia, at that time, were obviously in favour of support for the Tai-Tsing dynasty, and furthermore, the relations between our revolutionaries and their peoples were insignificant, and consequently we had no possibility of influencing their policy. Therefore, there remained only Japan, which was very close to us, and whose best sons not only expressed their sympathy with us, but had sacrificed their lives in the cause of the Revolution. The policy of the Japanese Government was, however, not quite clear in this question, and judging from previous experience one could suppose that it put up a negative attitude to our Revolution. Thus, on one occasion it expelled me from the country, and on another did not allow me to land in Japan.

Beginning with 1900, the Powers had not the right to act independently in China. There were six Powers who at that time took a very intimate part in the affairs of China. Of these, France and America took the side of the Revolution, Germany and Russia were opposed to the Revolution. England had not yet defined her policy, though her people also expressed its sympathy with the Revolution, and, while the Japanese Government was against the Revolution, the Japanese people sympathised with it.

Thus, the international situation was a question of life or death for the Chinese Revolution. The most important of all for us, at the moment, was the attitude of England, for we considered that if England took our side Japan would not delay in following her example. Therefore, I decided to leave for England.

When going through St. Louis, I read a newspaper statement to the effect that a revolution had broken out at Wuchang on the orders of Sun-Yat-Sen, and that in the proposed Republic Sun-Yat-Sen would be the President. After this I had to hide from the Press correspondents, as it turned out that rumour was in advance of fact.

Accompanied by comrade Chu-Cho-Wen, I continued my long journey to England. On arrival in New York, I received information that the comrades were making an attack on Canton, and I sent a telegram to Governor Chang-Ni-Isi proposing that he should surrender the city, in order to avoid bloodshed, and ordered the comrades to grant him his life, which was later on carried out.

On my arrival in England, I entered through my English friend into negotiations with the Banking Consortium of the Four Powers, with a view to stopping all loans for the Imperial Manchu House. The position was that the Consortium had already granted one loan of a hundred millions on the security of the Chuan-Hang Railway, and then a further loan of a hundred millions. On one of these loans the money had already been partly paid, but on the other, although the signature was appended, the bonds had not yet been issued. My intention was to secure the stoppage of payment on the loan which had been carried through, and to prevent the issue of bonds for the other loan. I knew that the settlement of this depended on the Foreign Secretary, and therefore I instructed the Director of the Wei-Hai-Wei Arsenal to enter into negotiations with the British Government on three questions, on the settlement of which I insisted. The first was the annulment of all loans to the Tai-Tsing dynasty. The second was to prevent Japan from helping the dynasty, and the third was to withdraw all orders prohibiting me from entering British territory, so that I could return to China more conveniently. Having received a favourable settlement of these questions from the British Government, I then turned to the Banking Consortium to secure a loan for the revolutionary Government. I received the following reply from the manager of the Consortium : " Since the Government has stopped the loans for the dynasty, our Consortium will grant these loans only to a firmly established and officially recognised Government. The Consortium proposes for the present to send a representative with you on your return, and when the official recognition of your Government takes place, it will be possible to open negotiations." This was all I could do during my stay in England. I then returned home through France, and during my passage through Paris met representatives of the French Opposition parties. I received expressions of sympathy from all, particularly from Premier Clemenceau. Thirty days after my departure from France I arrived at Shanghai. The Peace Conference of South and North was taking place at this time, but the Constitution of the future Republic was not yet determined.

Even before my arrival at Shanghai, all the foreign and Chinese newspapers were spreading widely the story that I was returning home with a large sum of money to help the Revolution. When I arrived at Shanghai, both my comrades and the reporters of the Foreign and Chinese newspapers expected this, but I replied that I had not brought with me a farthing: but had brought with me a revolutionary spirit, and that, until the aim of the Revolution had been achieved, there could be no question of peace conferences.

Soon after this the deputies from all the provinces of China, assembled in the city of Nanking, elected me Provisional President of China. In 1912 I assumed office, and ordered the proclamation of the Chinese Republic, the alteration of the lunar calendar, and the declaration of that year as the First Year of the Chinese Republic.

Thus thirty years passed as one day, and only after their completion did I achieve my principal aim, the aim of my life—the creation of the Chinese Republic.

APPENDIX I

"SAN-MIN-CHU" (THE THREE PRINCIPLES)[1]

COMRADES,

To-day, at the opening of our Executive session, the question involuntarily arises before me : what does our organisation represent ? This in brief is its history, and the principles which guide it.

Our Party was formed after the overthrow of the Tsing (Manchu) dynasty and the establishment of a republican form of Government. It has to play a tremendous part in the future of our country. From the time this Party was dissolved, China has been constantly in a state of disorder. It is, of course, natural that the reason for the disturbances and sufferings of the Chinese people was the dissolution of our Party. For many years we have fought, and are still fighting, against the traitors to the people who live to this day in the northern provinces of China, where the influence of our Party is very small : nevertheless, sooner or later the northerners will join us. In the south of China, in the sphere of influence of the Party, there is only the single province of Kwantung.

Our Party is revolutionary. In the second year after the establishment of the republican order, many of its members went abroad, where they worked energetically for the development of the revolutionary movement in

---

[1] A speech by Sun-Yat-Sen, delivered on March 6th, 1921, at a meeting of the Executive Committee of the Kuomintang at Canton.

China. Hence the name of the Party. While it was working in Tokyo, the Party was known as the " National League " : the difference of names, of course, does not alter the character and essence of the aims it pursues. Our Republic is already ten years old, but we still cannot look upon it as a fully perfected type, or consider that our aim has been achieved. Our work is not yet completed : we must continue the struggle.

Our Party is radically different from all the other parties of China. Thus, there was a party which strove for the overthrow of the Tsing dynasty and the establishment of another dynasty, Ming. Of course, the principles of this party were opposed to ours. When in the last years of the Tsing dynasty, we were forced to establish ourselves in Tokyo, we determined the following as the fundamental principles of our Party : nationalism, democracy and Socialism.

At that time, power in China was still in the hands of the Manchus, and the Revolution had only arrived at its first stage, nationalism, passing over the other two principles. " The Fivefold Constitution " has great importance for our country in the sense of establishing a firm and just form of government ; but, before the overthrow of the Tsing dynasty, many thought that the overthrow of that dynasty was the ultimate aim of our Party, and that thereafter China would proceed along the road of universal development and success. But has that proved to be the case ? It is now clear that the reason for all that has happened is that our comrades despised—in the name of nationalism—the other two principles of democracy and Socialism. This once again proves that our work did not conclude with the overthrow of the Tsing dynasty. We must firmly know and remember that, so long as all three principles have not been carried into real life (even if one of them had been completely realised), there can be no stable conditions of existence. Furthermore, in fact, our nationalism has not yet been completely realised. The principles of President Lincoln completely coincide with mine. He said : " A government of the people, elected by the people and for the people." These principles have served as the maximum of achievement for Europeans as well as Americans. Words which have the same sense can be found in China : I have translated them : " nationalism, democracy and Socialism." Of course, there can be other interpretations. The wealth and power of the United States are a striking example of the results of great men's teachings in that country. I am glad to observe that my principles, too, are shared by the greatest political minds abroad and are not in contradiction to all the world's democratic schools of thought.

I now wish to speak of nationalism.

(1) *Nationalism*

What meaning do we impart to the word " nationalism " ? With the establishment of the Manchu dynasty in China, the people remained under an incredible yoke for over two hundred years. Now that dynasty has been overthrown, and the people, it would seem, ought to enjoy complete freedom. But does the Chinese people enjoy all the blessings of liberty ? No. Then what is the reason ? Why, that our Party has as yet far from fulfilled its appointed tasks, and has carried out only the negative part of its work, without doing anything of its positive work.

Since the end of the great European War, the world position has sharply changed : the eyes of the whole world are now turned to the Far East, particularly to China. Strictly speaking, amongst all the nations of the Far East only Siam and Japan are completely independent. China, vast territorially and exceeding dozens of times in population the independent countries, is yet in effect only semi-independent. What is the reason ?

After the overthrow of the monarchy and the establishment of the republican system in the territory populated by the five nationalities (Chinese, Manchus, Mongols, Tartars and Tibetans), a vast number of reactionary and religious elements appeared. And here lies the root of the evil. Numerically, these nationalities stand as follows : there are several million Tibetans, less than a million Mongols, about ten million Tartars, and the most insignificant number of Manchus. Politically their distribution is as follows : Manchuria is in the sphere of Japanese influence, Mongolia, according to recent reports, is under the influence of Russia, and Tibet is the booty of Great Britain. These races have not sufficient strength for self-defence, but they might unite with the Chinese to form a single State.

There are 400 million Chinese : if they cannot organise a single nation, a united State, this is their disgrace, and moreover a proof that we have not given complete effect even to the first principle, and that we must fight for a long while yet to carry out our tasks to the full. We shall establish an united Chinese Republic in order that all the peoples—Manchus, Mongols, Tibetans, Tartars and Chinese—should constitute a single powerful nation. As an example of what I have described, I can refer to the people of the United States of America, constituting one great and terrible whole, but in reality consisting of many separate nationalities : Germans, Dutch, English, French, etc. The United States are an example of a united nation. Such a nationalism is possible, and we must pursue it.

The name " Republic of Five Nationalities " exists only because there exists a certain racial distinction which distorts the meaning of a single Republic. We must facilitate the dying out of all names of individual peoples inhabiting China, i.e. Manchus, Tibetans, etc. In this respect we must follow the example of the United States of America, i.e. satisfy the demands and requirements of all races and unite them in a single cultural and political whole, to constitute a single nation with such a name, for example, as " Chunhua " (China—in the widest application of the name). Organise the nation, the State.

Or take another case of a nation of mingled races— Switzerland. It is situated in the heart of Europe : on one side it borders on France, on another on Germany, on a third, Italy. Not all the parts of this State have a common tongue, yet they constitute one nation. And only the wise cultural and political life of Switzerland makes its people of many races united and strong. All this is the consequence of the citizens of this Republic enjoying equal and direct electoral rights. Regarding this country from the aspect of international policy, we see that it was the first to establish equal and direct electoral rights for all the population. This is an example of " nationalism."

But let us imagine that the work of uniting all the tribes who inhabit China has been completed, and one nation, " Chunhua," has been formed. Still the object has not been achieved. There are still many peoples suffering from unjust treatment : the Chinese people must assume the mission of setting free these people from their yoke, in the sense of direct aid for them or uniting them under the banner of a single Chinese nation. This would give them the opportunity to enjoy the feeling of equality of man and man, and of a just international attitude, i.e. that which was expressed in the declaration of the American President Wilson by the words " self-determination of nations." Up to the moment of reaching this political stage, our work cannot be considered as finished. Everyone who wishes to join China must be considered Chinese. This is the meaning of nationalism—but " positive " nationalism, and to this we must give special attention.

(2) *Democracy*

I have already said that in Switzerland democracy has reached its highest point of development : but at the same time the system of representation prevailing there does not constitute real democracy, and only the direct right of the citizen fully answers to the requirements of democracy. Although revolutions took place at various times in France, America and England, and resulted in the establishment of the existing representative system, nevertheless that system does not mean direct and equal rights for all citizens, such as we are fighting for to-day. The most essential of such rights are : the franchise for all citizens : the right of recall (the officials elected by the people can be dismissed by them at will): the right of referendum (if the legislative body passes a law contrary to the wishes of the citizens, the latter may reject the law) : the right of initiative (the citizens may propose draft laws, to be carried and adopted by the legislative body).

These four fundamental clauses constitute the basis of what I call " direct electoral rights."

(3) *Socialism*

The theory of Socialism has become known in China comparatively recently. Its chief advocates usually limit their knowledge of this tendency to a few empty words, without having any definite programme. By long study I have formed a concrete view of this question. The essence of Socialism amounts to solving the problem of land and capital.

Above I have set forth the general main idea of the " three principles." The efforts of the whole world, including the Chinese people, are directed to this aim, and I say that our Party must immediately set about carrying these principles into effect.

Summing up the above, I want also to make a few additional observations.

(1) *Nationalism.*—Since the overthrow of the Tsing dynasty, we have carried out only one part of our obligations : we have fulfilled only our passive duty, but have done nothing in the realm of positive work. We must raise the prestige of the Chinese people, and unite all the races inhabiting China to form one Chinese people in eastern Asia, a Chinese National State.

(2) *Democracy.*—To bring about this ideal we must first of all adopt all the four points of direct electoral rights : universal suffrage, the referendum, the initiative and the right of recall.

(3) *Socialism*—Here I have my plan.

The first task of my plan is to bring about the proportional distribution of the land. During my stay at Nanking (as Provisional President), I tried to carry out this proposal, but my desire was not fulfilled, as I was not understood. Social questions arise from the inequality between rich and poor. What do we understand by inequality ? In ancient times, although there was a distinction between rich and poor, it was not so sharp as to-day. To-day the rich own all the land, while the poor have not even a little plot. The reason for this inequality is the difference in productive power. For example, in ancient times timber-cutters used axes, knives, etc., for their work, whereas to-day industry is greatly developed, machines have replaced human labour, and the result is that a much greater quantity of products is secured at the expense of much less human energy.

Take another example, from the sphere of agriculture. In ancient times only human labour was employed in this sphere ; but with the introduction of ploughing with horses and oxen, the process of tilling became more speedy and greatly reduced human effort. In Europe and America electrical energy is now used to till the soil, which affords the opportunity of ploughing in the best possible way more than a thousand acres a day, thus eliminating the use of horses and oxen. This has created a truly amazing difference, expressed by the ratio of a thousand to one. If we take the means of communication, however, we see that the introduction of steamships and railways has made communications more than a thousand times more rapid in comparison with human energy.

Those who discuss the question of the brotherhood of peoples in America and Europe have in view only two problems—labour and capital ; but European conditions are very different from our own. The thing is that in Europe and America all their misfortunes arise from an

extremely unfair distribution of products, whereas in
China there is general poverty, since there are no large
capitalists. But this, of course, should not serve as a
reason for not advocating Socialism : this would be a
great mistake. If we see mistakes in Europe and America,
we are bound to correct them : disproportion in the
distribution of products, both in America and in Europe,
are a bad example for us. Therefore I agitate for
Socialism—the socialisation of land and capital.

First we shall speak of the socialisation of land. The
land systems of Europe and America are very different.
In England up to this day the feudal system of land-
holding has survived, whereas in the United States all
the land is private property. But my social theory
advocates the proportionalisation of the land, as a means
of providing against future evils. We can see the latter
beginning even at the present day. Take what is going
on under our very eyes since the reorganisation of the
Canton municipality : communications have improved,
and in consequence the price of land along the embank-
ment and in other most thickly populated districts has
begun to increase daily, some estates selling for tens of
thousands of dollars per mu. And all this belongs to
private persons, living by the labour of others.

The old Chinese land system partially conforms to the
principle of proportionalisation of land. In the event of
this principle being applied, the two following conditions
must be observed : taxation according to the value of
the land, and compensation according to declared value.
In China up to this day the so-called three-grade system
of collection of land taxes has been preserved, but,
owing to the weak development of transport and industry,
land values were not so high in the past as they are

233

to-day. Well-developed means of communication and developing industry have led, owing to the maintenance of the old system, to an extremely unequal rise in the value of the land. There are, for example, lands worth 2000 dollars per mu, while there are also lands worth 20,000 dollars per mu, while between these two extremes of values there are a large number of the most varying values. But if taxes continue to be collected on the old system, both the tax collectors and taxpayers will be put in such a position that dishonest collectors and landowners can make easy profits thereby.

Therefore if we want to abolish this evil and introduce the graduation of taxes, we must adopt the following method : to collect one per cent. of the value of the land. For example, if a given piece of land is worth 2000 dollars, its owner pays 20 dollars. The collection of further taxes will depend on an increase in the value of the land. The process of State purchase of the land must begin with the establishment of its definite value. In England, at one time, special offices for collection of land tax and purchase of land were set up, which fixed definite assessments : these methods are not suitable for introduction in China. In my opinion, it is much more profitable and certain to leave it to the landowner himself to determine and fix the value and the tax, and to inform accordingly the Government department in charge of these matters.

The question arises : will not the landowner communicate a smaller value for his land, and thus pay a smaller tax ? But if we adopt the system of compensation for lands according to their value, all illegal activities must disappear of themselves. For example, there is a piece of land of one mu, worth 1000 dollars, for which the

"SAN-MIN-CHU"

owner must pay 10 dollars yearly in to the tax office. He may declare that the value of his land is only 100 dollars, and thus pay only one dollar ; but the application of the principle whereby the Government can compulsorily purchase his land at its declared value obliges the owner to declare its real value, as otherwise he runs the risk of being left without his land. If these two methods are applied, the proportionalisation of land will achieve itself ; we can leave other processes on one side for the time being. Thus I have discussed the land question. There still remains the issue of how to settle the problem of capital. Last year I published a book entitled : *The International Development of China.* In this book I discussed the question of utilising foreign capital for the purpose of developing Chinese industry and commerce. Look at the Pekin-Hankow and Pekin-Mukden railways, and also at the Tientsin-Pukow line, built by foreign capital and yielding enormous profits. At the present time the total length of the Chinese railways is 5000–6000 miles, and their profits amount to 70–80 millions—more even than the land tax. But if the total length is increased to 50 or 60 thousand miles, the profits will also increase considerably. My opinion about the application of foreign capital to our industry is the following : all branches of our industry, for example mining, which represent, with any management worth its salt, profitable undertakings, are awaiting foreign capital.

When I speak of a loan in this connection, I mean the procuring of various machines and other necessary appliances for our industry. For example, after the construction of the Pekin-Hankow railway, the profits of which were enormous, the foreigners would have given us the chance to acquire it, with its future profit-making possibilities. These were so great that we could have completed the Pekin-Kalgan line, which now reaches Sunyang. In brief, we can easily incur debt to foreign capital, but the question is—how shall we utilise it, productively or otherwise ?

There are also other questions of which I must speak. The British and American diplomats are undoubtedly a skilful race, but still the spectre of social revolution is extremely menacing in these countries. Why ? Because the principles of Socialism have not been fully realised there.

We must admit that the degree of sacrifice required for the social revolution will be higher than for the political. The Revolution of 1911 and the overthrow of the Manchus only partially realised the principle of nationalism, while neither the theory of democracy nor the theory of Socialism left any impression. But we must strive our utmost not only to secure the triumph of our first Party principle, but, in accordance with modern world ideas, to develop if possible the principles of democracy, which are also old principles of our Party. Although both England and America are politically developed, political authority there still remains in the hands, not of the people as a whole, but of a political party.

I remember that, on my return to Kwantung, a well-known Hong Kong paper stated the meaning of our return to be that Kwantung was governed, not by the people of the province, but by a " Party." There was a certain point in this declaration. At all events, I was pleased to hear a confirmation that it was governed by a " Party," as the same was true of England and America. If we succeed in achieving our Party ends, this will undoubtedly be a great achievement for the people of Kwantung. We must energetically set about organising, explaining our principles, spreading them far and wide. If we want to awaken others, we must first of all wake up ourselves. Now there is a committee of the Kuomintang at Canton, where propaganda will be concentrated. In this respect there will be no limitations. We shall soon find that the province of Kwantung will not only be the soil on which our principles will grow into reality, but will be the birthplace of the idea of democracy and its practical realisation. From here these principles and their realisation will spread all over China. The people of the Yangtse and Yellow River valleys will follow our example. The haste of our action is explained by the fact that the people which has been actually living in the Republic set up by itself over ten years ago is quite ignorant of what the word means : the explanation of the significance of the Republic must be our task.

During the great European War, President Wilson put forward the watchword : " self-determination of peoples." This corresponds to our Party principle of " nationalism." After the Peace Conference at Versailles, a number of small but independent republics were formed, living without any common tie. This must clearly show you the principal tendency in the modern life of nations. Now the time is approaching to carry into effect our great principles of nationalism, democracy and Socialism. Only by the transformation of all three principles into reality can our people live and develop freely. But the explanation and application of these principles depends very largely on the display of your forces and the degree of energy shown in your propaganda.

We now have a favourable occasion for the propaganda of our ideas : the whole Kwantung Province, with its population of 30 millions, is in our hands. We must immediately tackle the work of explaining in detail to all citizens the essential principles of our Party programme.

APPENDIX II

" THE FIVEFOLD CONSTITUTION "

(*A Speech by Sun-Yat-Sen*)

COMRADES,

The subject of this speech will be the " Fivefold Constitution," which is the fruit exclusively of my work and hitherto has been unknown. You know that the whole world strives for the establishment of a constitutional system ; this term must be known to many representatives of the Chinese people, which for the last ten or twenty years has been living an intense political life. But what is a constitution ? A constitutional order is a system in which all political authority is divided into several component parts, independent of one another in their work. The constitutions of other countries are divided only into three component parts, but not into five. The constitution of five component parts is the fruit of my labours alone. From the moment of its appearance, very few have understood its purpose. I shall try to explain it.

Ten years ago I spoke on this subject, and apparently my audience were very inattentive. In all other countries there exists the so-called threefold constitution, and therefore it was very strange for them to hear of a new form, and they decided that it was purely the result of my fantasy. But I based the idea of my work on a very solid foundation. I studied the history of revolutions for over thirty years. After an unsuccessful revolt in

Kwantung, I went abroad, and seriously began the study of the problem of why great political movements in various countries were unsuccessful. My object was to create the foundation for the future system of government of China.

I succeeded in studying all these questions seriously and in detail. After the successful conclusion of the revolt of the United States of America, the colonists who had secured complete independence of Great Britain laid at the foundation of their system of government a threefold constitution, the clauses and articles of which are distinguished by their exactness and clearness. This constitution is called in the political world a " written Constitution." Many countries followed the example of the U.S.A., and laid this constitution at the foundation of the laws of their country. I studied the American constitution, which from the moment of its appearance was recognised as a model, not only by the American people itself, but also by the British statesmen, who saw in it something superior to all other forms of constitution in other countries. I was very careful and painstaking about the study of this constitution, in order to secure a reply to the question : was it perfect or not ? The result of my work was the conviction that it suffers from many defects. Moreover, the opinion of some European and American scholars about the American Constitution coincides with mine in many respects. To-day very many feel the imperfectness of the American Constitution. This is because all that was good and correct a hundred or two hundred years ago is by no means suitable to-day. From this angle, and also thanks to my intensive study of the question, I decided that these imperfections must be eliminated. The American students of political science are of the same opinion. Undoubtedly, the perfection of a constitution is not an easy matter. How is it to be done ? We have at our disposal neither materials nor the necessary books.

I remember that a certain American professor wrote a book, entitled, *Liberty*, in which he develops the idea that the threefold constitution does not correspond to the spirit of the times, and therefore he advises the introduction of a fourth component part, the " power of punishment " of members of Parliament, which must be absolutely independent in its actions. He thinks that if Parliament possesses this power, cunning members of Parliament will abuse it and will always place the Government in a very difficult position. But his opinion also is not quite correct. In America there are a fair number of people who feel the imperfection of their Constitution, and seek a method of improving it. But the method indicated is also imperfect. Why ? Because in the United States all public servants are elected by the people, but, in view of the existence of many difficulties in popular elections, and other grave defects, the method of limiting elections of officials is applied : the vote belongs only to people possessing certain privileges. Such a privilege is the possession of a certain amount of property, which gives its owner the right to vote. Undoubtedly such a form of restriction in elections at the present day is in contradiction to the spirit of equality, and gives rise to the vast growth of corruption. Moreover, in such a system we do not know who should be elected. Undoubtedly, those who are elected should possess certain qualities, but the right to vote should be extended to all citizens of the Republic. Such a system is called " Universal Suffrage." In all countries we

observe to-day a struggle going on for this object. This
is a very good method, but who should be elected ?

It is not such a simple thing as to say that, once you
have property, you can vote and be elected. I think
that every worker in the public service, and every worker
of the legislative institutions, ought to have certain
knowledge and aptness for his work. But if he has neither
knowledge nor aptitude, but only property, this is in
contradiction to the requirements of the age. Let us suppose that we have fifty men who possess the necessary
knowledge and qualifications. We must select those
whom we need. But who can tell us that they are the
most suitable for the work ? Previously, there existed
in China the method of examination for the Civil Service.
But the old Chinese method was useless during the
time of the dynasty, because the Emperor in those days
was only concerned with finding the people he required
to rule the country. However, this method is extremely
useful and necessary for the Republic, as the whole
people is unable to assemble to manage the affairs of the
country. The examination section, therefore, is the fifth
component part of which I have spoken. All this was the
result of my protracted and concentrated labours ; I am
certain that practice will show the complete suitability
of this system.

The " United League," while it was still in Tokyo,
accepted the scheme of the " Three Principles " and the
" Fivefold Constitution " as its programme. We decided
at that time that, after the successful completion of the
revolutionary insurrection, the constitution must be
applied in practice. We did not imagine that, after the
overthrow of the Manchu dynasty, anyone would take
advantage of the difficult circumstances. Everyone

thought that the very fact of the overthrow of the Manchu dynasty would be a proof that all would be organised as the people desired. The result is the existence of the so-called " Republican System " in China, which has not only not applied the principles for which the best sons of China struggled, but on the whole has even made matters worse. The reason for this must be clear to you, even without my explanations. We must immediately bend all our efforts to applying the "Fivefold Constitution" which will lay the foundation for a strong and healthy form of government. We must have a good Constitution and then we shall be able to build up a real Republic.

From the time that the " Fivefold Constitution " made its first appearance, no one has studied its essence sufficiently to understand it properly and agree with it. I remember that, about twenty years ago, there was a Chinese student who had passed through the Chinese Faculty of Law. He wished to supplement his knowledge in this sphere and study his subject more deeply, and for this purpose went to a famous American University. I met him in New York and asked what subjects he was studying in particular. He replied that he had taken the question of Constitutions as a special subject for study. I then told him of my scheme of a " Fivefold Constitution" and discussed it with him for about two weeks. In the end he declared that the " Fivefold Constitution " was much better than any other. I begged him to study this question seriously in the University. Later on he completed his studies, and received the degree of Doctor ; thus his knowledge must have been very extensive. Having passed out of the University, he travelled in England, France and Germany to study constitutions in practice. after the first successful revolution he returned to China

He then declared that he had not met with such a constitution in other countries, and therefore considered that the possibility of our applying it in practice was extremely small. When I heard this declaration, I knew it was mistaken. Yet all our comrades at that time thought that the opinion expressed by this doctor was right; "there is no such constitution in any other country, and therefore it must be bad and does not deserve attention."

When I was at Nanking, my professor in jurisprudence was a Japanese Doctor of Laws ; I discussed very many questions with him. After the failure of the second revolution, I went to Japan and again met him. He asked me what I called the " Fivefold Constitution." I explained it to him in detail, and after we had lived together for about three months he at last grasped it.

Thus both doctors, in the long run, declared that this constitutional theory has nothing in common with the constitutions of other countries, and therefore the question must remain open. Seeing such a cautious attitude, I was nevertheless convinced that in the course of time, whether it be after several hundreds or even thousands of years, this Constitution will be adopted.

We strive to make China a powerful and glorious country, but how can we bring this about ? I think that the path must not be very difficult. This path is the application of the " Fivefold Constitution." Over twenty years have now passed since the day when I spoke on this theme, on the anniversary of the " Min-Pao " in Tokyo ; yet still the number of supporters of this Constitution is extremely small. We must welcome every desire to become acquainted with this question. But if we attempt to draw the picture of this Constitution in all its details, two weeks will be insufficient, for the theme is too great. Let us consider, at any rate, why we require this Constitution. If we desire to understand this, we must first make a review of political history for the space of several thousand years past. In political history there exists two tendencies ; one, " Liberty," the other, " Order." In political history, just as in physics, there are two forces, centrifugal and centripetal. The tendency of the centrifugal force is extension without, the tendency of the centripetal is collection around the centre. If the centrifugal force is stronger than any object, the latter will break up into dust ; but if the centripetal force is the stronger, the object will only become slightly smaller and more compressed. It is necessary that these two forces should be equal. The same applies to " Liberty " and " Order." If the boundaries of " Liberty " are widely extended, there is a possibility that anarchy will arise ; but if " Order " takes first place, there will be the sway of absolutism. Political changes for the last few thousand years are the result of the conflict of these two forces.

The history of China began with the dynasties of Tan and Yu : this period is called the " Golden Age." The history of China is the history of the movement from liberty to absolutism, while the history of Europe is the history of the movement from absolutism to liberty. Our people enjoyed liberty too long, and began to grow tired of it, and finally destroyed it. Then selfish emperors and kings took advantage of the opportunity to assume the toga of absolutism : the autocracy of the Tsing and Tang dynasties began. The political history of other countries goes from absolutism to liberty : in earlier times people suffered great misery, and therefore in those

MEMOIRS OF A CHINESE REVOLUTIONARY

countries the saying arose : " Either liberty or death."
Thus we can see the terrible meaning of absolutism at
that time.

The history of Chinese political life goes from liberty
to absolutism. The Chinese people in ancient times
independently cultivated their fruit and dug wells for
their water, and were completely free. This is what the
philosopher, Lao-tze said : " A country must be governed
without interference." This is the popular conception
of liberty. At that time the people enjoyed complete
liberty, but did not know its value. This tradition has
been maintained up to the present day. The apathy of
the Chinese to liberty is a source of constant wonder to
the Europeans. The character of European history is
quite the reverse. From the moment of the fall of the
Roman Empire, Europe was divided into a number of
countries, the nations of which were in the position of
slaves. During the last few centuries wars for liberty
have gone on.

Whenever I have spoken about revolution, I have never
confused this with the idea of winning liberty : the Chinese
people thinks only of a complete political change, but does
not connect this at all with the idea of liberty. The
Chinese Emperors only demanded that the people should
pay taxes and keep the peace. Hence it is clear why
Europe criticises the Chinese people for a complete failure
to understand the term "liberty." The Europeans do
not enjoy complete liberty, and therefore fight to win it.
But the Chinese have enjoyed unlimited liberty, and
therefore do not know the meaning of the word.

These two tendencies of political history, absolutism,
and liberty, are the distinguishing features separating
China from Europe. But in political history there are

also two classes of people : those who govern and those who are governed. Here is what one philosopher said on this subject : " There are men occupied with gymnastics of the mind, there are men occupied with gymnastics of the body. The first will rule, the second will be ruled." Those who will rule must have knowledge, while those who will be ruled must not have knowledge. The people of ancient times were like children, thinking only of who should direct them. But now the people have grown up and understand that this distinction between rulers and ruled must be abolished. In Europe, the monarchical system and its Emperors were overthrown only during recent centuries, and the people enjoy comparative liberty. My " Fivefold Constitution " strives to destroy this distinction, thereby serving as the true and real path to the realisation of the principles of democracy.

Now let us speak of the place of origin of constitutions A constitution was first created in England. From the time of the Great English Revolution, the power of the monarch gradually declined, and finally became a pure political tradition, like the " division of the three powers." But in reality the English do not know that these " three powers " were divided : they possess a natural feeling of love for liberty, and act as seems best to them.

Three hundred years ago there was a famous French scholar, Montesquieu, who published a book called *The Spirit of Laws*, which set out the theory of the division of the three powers, and pointed out that the legislative, executive and judicial powers should be completely independent one of the other. But thanks to the great development of her political parties, England changed her forms of government only gradually, and now her government is not one of free, independent and separate powers, but a single authority. The modern political system in England is that of the complete dictatorship of Parliament, the complete authority of a single party which governs the country. The system of government of the United States of America, on the other hand, is based on the theory of the division of three powers formulated by Montesquieu, and is expressed in the exact forms of a written constitution. Yet Montesquieu himself based his theory of the division of three powers on the political traditions of England. Later, the reforms in Japan and the revolutions in other Countries took as the basis of their constitution the Constitution of the United States. The English Constitution is not formulated in documents, whereas the American constitution is expressed in a formal way in documents. Therefore, the English Constitution is still called " elastic," while the American is " strict " and " exact."

England is governed by individual persons, while the U.S.A. are governed by laws, although England is the country where there first appeared a constitution, though not drawn up in exact words. Our old Chinese system of government is a system of three powers, just like the English.

The Old Chinese System of Government.	*The Constitutions of other Countries.*
Power of Punishment. Power of the Emperor. Power of Examination. Judicial. Administrative. Legislative.	Judicial Power. Administrative Power. Legislative Power. Power of Examination. Power of Punishment.

According to the above diagram, the Chinese system of government includes the power of examination, the power of punishment and the power of the Emperor, which includes legislative, judicial and administrative departments. The system of examinations is very valuable. It used to be distinguished for its accuracy, absence of bribes and freedom from personal influence : but later this strictness gradually began to be relaxed. As for the power of punishment, there were special officials in control of it. In the event of the Emperor's actions being wrong, he too was subjected to punishment by this power, which insisted on punishment, even though this were death. Thus this system deserves approval.

There is an American professor, Burgess, who has written a book entitled *Liberty and Government*, in which he says that the power of punishment in China is the best example of a compromise between liberty and government. The Chinese people have spoken little of liberty : the extreme of liberty is anarchism. The reason for the constant discussion of anarchism in Europe is its comparative newness there. The first known anarchist was the French thinker and philosopher, Proudhon, and then the Russian, Bakunin : the representative of anarchism at the present day was the Russian philosopher, Kropotkin, who died recently. Many have engaged in concentrated study of this tendency in political thought, simply because it was still quite new. It is laughable when people speak of Chinese students who study this theory and advocate it, trying not to fall behind the fashion, without speaking of whether they understand it or not. In essence, the theory of anarchism was known in China several thousand years ago, when many were greatly interested in it. Is not the theory of Hung and Lao anarchism ? I repeat that people have talked of anarchism in China for several thousand years : and it is only because the Chinese youth do not understand this that they fail to realise that such propaganda is quite unnecessary at the present time.

I have already said that both political tendencies, liberty and absolutism, must come to a compromise in order that neither should go to an extreme, like the centrifugal and centripetal forces. To speak only of the centrifugal or the centripetal force is undoubtedly wrong. We must speak of both. Any opinion of one side alone will never be successful. The equality of both forces and the combination of both tendencies constitute the promise of a great future for mankind. The work of the Constitution is like the work of a machine : I emphasise that the Government is a machine. I may then be told that such an illustration is rather strange. But you know that there are machines for working up different raw materials : the same applies to the mechanism of human affairs. Law is the mechanism of human affairs. The Constitution is a great machine—the machine of compromise between liberty and government.

At the beginning of our Revolution I put forward the idea of the " three principles " i.e. nationalism, democracy and Socialism. These are the same words as were uttered by the President of the United States, Lincoln : " Government of the people, by the people, and for the people." Men must govern themselves, and then they will be completely satisfied. If they cannot govern themselves, they cannot be satisfied. If we desire to overthrow the system of government of those who have developed their minds over those who have been developed only physically, we must bear in mind that the human will can deal even with the heavens. There are in the world horses which can travel hundreds of miles a day, birds which can rise almost to the skies, fish which can swim at the very bottom of the sea—which man cannot naturally do. But if we wish to travel hundreds of miles in a day, or to fly in the air as high as a bird, or to swim in the sea, can we do this ? We can, if we have machines. If we take an automobile, we can traverse a distance of more than a thousand miles in a day. By using an aeroplane, we can reach the loftiest heights. With the help of submarines, we can descend to the bottom of the sea. This is what the human will and ideas can do. Formerly there were Greeks who were capable of marching hundreds of miles in a day : they of course were born with such a natural endurance and capacity for marching which is very rare. But now we have machines, with the help of which we can very easily obtain that which in former times demanded vast energy.

Let us go on to the question of democracy, which for the people is a machine wherewith to fly, run, swim and do all else that it pleases. But what kind of machine is it ? This machine is a constitution.

The Constitution of Five Grades (or Authorities).

| Legislative. | Judicial. | Executive. | Punishment. | Examining. |

This five-grade or Fivefold Constitution is our automobile, our submarine and our aeroplane. It is divided into the following authorities : legislative, judicial, administrative or executive, punishment and examining for civil servants—all completely independent of one another. It deprives the Emperor of his power and takes legislative, judicial and administrative authority away from him, making them quite independent. At the head of the administration stands the President ; at the head

251

of the legislative machine is Parliament ; at the head of the judiciary is a judge.

Every worker in State employment must first of all pass certain examinations. I remember that, when I arrived in Canton, many people asked me to give them posts in the Civil Service. The Government needed competent and experienced workers. But I knew none. Perhaps there were experienced old workers amongst these persons, but without a certain test of their knowledge I could do nothing. In such a case this authority is very useful. Many skilled people have been unknown to a large section of society because they were never subjected to examination. And sometimes it happens that ignorant and almost illiterate people achieve high posts, and thereby only awaken and develop sullen hostility in the hearts of the people. Thus we see that the examining power is a very essential and important link in the State machinery. Without this link it is as though we were without a conductor. Only with this system can we have experienced civil servants.

This system was adopted in practice by England a fairly long time ago, and by America about twenty or thirty years ago. All this was borrowed from China. The Chinese system of examinations is the best in the world, and all countries now use it.

Above I mentioned that the legislative authority is headed by Parliament, the executive by the President, the judicial by a judge ; the examining and punishing authorities are also controlled by appropriate persons. When I was at Nanking, I requested the Senate to adopt the Fivefold Constitution. But they did not understand it, as it cut completely across their personal points of view. The Fivefold Constitution, the fruit of my own

" THE FIVEFOLD CONSTITUTION "

labours, is a vast machine. If you wish to travel hundreds of miles in a day, you take an automobile or an aeroplane ; if you wish to manage a country, you must use a machine which you can control.

The State Machine.

People's Conference.   Every district has one delegate.

Government.

| Punishing authority. | Judicial authority. | Executive authority. | Legislative authority. | Examinatory authority. |

Minister of Justice.   Minister of Finance.   Minister for Interior.   Minister of Foreign Affairs.   Minister of Education.

Provincial authority.

District authority.   Direct right of citizens.

Initiative.   Right of Recall.   Referendum.   Direct electoral rights.

This is the machinery for governing the country. Beside the Fivefold Constitution, a very important part is the direct right of citizens in local government. Direct right is the true " rights of man." It has four forms : electoral, the right of recall, the initiative and the referendum. If the Fivefold Constitution can be compared to a vast machine, the direct right of citizens is the key to the machine. If citizens have the right of election, they should also have the right of dismissing the officials whom they elect. If citizens know of the existence of useful laws, which for some reason cannot pass the legislature, they should be able as a community to adopt them. Such a right is called the right of referendum.

In our Provisional Constitution there is no definite paragraph about the rights of citizens referred to above. In the Constitution adopted at Nanking there is only one paragraph : " The Chinese Republic belongs only to the Chinese people as a whole." This was my proposal. The rest was not concerted with my opinion, and I cannot be held responsible for it. The day before yesterday I spoke to you about the general principles of our Provisional Provincial Assembly ; I trust that the members of that Assembly will demand of the Canton Parliament that it adopt the Fivefold Constitution as the foundation of the Government of China.